Eine bestimmte Architektur kann nur ihre eigenen Realitäten in sich tragen, denn die Konzeption, auf der sie beruht, besteht gerade darin, sich nicht auf die Baukunst an sich zu berufen, sondern eine andere auszugestalten, ausgehend von allen möglichen Gegebenheiten, die auf den ersten Blick nichts mit ihr zu tun haben. Wirft ein solches Werk für den Betrachter Fragen auf, so bedeutet es für den Gestalter eine Situation der langanhaltenden Spannung: Erst muß der Bau vollendet, dann angenommen und schließlich erlebt werden. Das Erleben eines neuen Objekts erfordert aber einige Anpassungen. Wie geht man an ein Objekt heran, das eine neue Sprache spricht? Mit alten Gewohnheiten? Oder ergeben sich auf «natürliche» Weise neue? Und wie macht man die einem Raum eingeprägte Bedeutung spürbar, wenn sich in diesem Raum jeder gleich einem Elektron auf Silicium seinen eigenen Weg bahnt, seinen zum fragilen Moment des Besuchs für einen Augenblick sich vergegenwärtigenden Geschichtssplitter hervorbringt – das, was man erkennt, was man spürt, ohne bewußt wahrzunehmen, also all jene aufblitzenden Momente, die die Erinnerung an einen Schauplatz bilden, das Vorbeieilen unbestimmter Formen in sehr kurzer Zeit? Da wird die Architektur nicht mehr als rettende Theorie entschlüsselt; sie drängt sich vielmehr auf als eine, sich zuweilen überlagernde, Abfolge von Bildern. Im Gegensatz zum Text kennen Bilder aber keinerlei gemeinsame Semiotik, sondern jedes einzelne entwickelt ein vielfältiges, bis ins Unendliche eigenständiges System. Beim Abbilden eines konkreten Gegenstands reduziert sich dessen Bedeutung, wodurch eine andere aufscheint. Dem Gestalter dieses Bauwerks – das mehr aus Fragen denn aus Gewißheiten besteht – stellt sich also die Aufgabe, einen Argumentationskatalog aus der eigentlichen architektonischen Substanz zu erarbeiten. Deshalb sucht er unerbittlich nach der Bedeutung seines Werks, unter anderem in den folgenden fotografischen Wiedergaben, – und es kommt so gut wie nie vor, daß er sie nicht findet. Jean Nouvel zeichnet nicht, er trägt seine Visionen vor, um den grausamen Augenblick, in dem das Konzept Form annimmt, in dem sich eine Gestalt herauskristallisiert, so lange wie möglich hinauszuschieben. Muß er das, was sich bei ihm herauskristallisiert hat, heute auf seine Weise zeigen? Muß er seinen Träumen weiter nachhängen, seine Hoffnungen weiter hegen…? Dort, wo der Entwurf rätselhaft ist und einer Interpretation bedarf, müßte es die Fotografie nicht minder sein, insofern sie einer anderen kulturellen Ebene angehört: jener des klaren Zaubers der Genauigkeit, wo die Ausführung im Handumdrehen und in irreversibler Ausprägung erfolgt. Ein solches «Abbild der Realität» ist zugleich unerträglich, faszinierend und schwer zu meistern. Jean Nouvel hat hier der von ihm erbauten Wirklichkeit ein paar Ideen-Bilder entlockt, damit wir besser nachvollziehen können, worauf seine Konzeption von Architektur beruht. **Hubert Tonka**

jean nouvel luzern

concert hall
konzertsaal
salle de concert

photographs by jean nouvel

edition architekturgalerie luzern (editor)

birkhäuser publishers
basel • boston • berlin

Une certaine architecture ne peut trouver qu'en elle ses réalités puisque la conception qui la porte est de ne pas se référer à l'art architectural lui-même, mais, justement, à en façonner un autre à partir de toutes sortes de choses ne lui appartenant pas à première vue. Si cette architecture est une interrogation pour celui qui la perçoit elle est une inquiétude pour celui qui la conçoit; pour lui l'attente est longue. L'édifice doit être achevé, reçu puis vécu. Le vécu d'un nouvel objet ne va pas sans exiger quelques ajustements. Comment aborder un objet au langage nouveau? Avec les anciennes habitudes ou en forge-t-il «naturellement» de nouvelles? Comment faire ressentir le sens incrusté dans un espace où chacun, comme un électron sur du silicium, crée son parcours individuel, son fragment d'histoire momentanée dans le moment fragile de la visite, de ce que l'on repère, de ce que l'on ressent sans percevoir consciemment, enfin tous ces instants brefs qui inscrivent le souvenir d'une scène le passage dans un court instant de temps de formes incertaines. L'architecture n'est plus décryptée comme une théorie salvatrice, elle s'impose, plutôt, comme une suite, parfois superposée, d'images. Mais l'image a contrario du texte ne connaît aucune sémiologie partagée, chacune développe un système composite, autonome à l'infini. La mise en image d'un objet réel opère par réduction de sens faisant apparaître un autre. Donc la tâche du concepteur de cette architecture, plus faite d'interrogations que de certitudes, est d'élaborer des argumentaires à partir de la matière même de l'architecture, pour cela, entre autre, il pourchasse le sens de son ouvrage dans les représentations photographiques qui vont être divulguées – il est moins que rare qu'il ne le trouve pas.   Jean Nouvel ne dessine pas, il conte ses visions afin de reculer le plus possible l'instant cruel où le concept va devenir forme, se cristallise en une figure. A-t-il besoin, aujourd'hui, de montrer à sa façon ses cristallisations, poursuivre ses songes et prolonger ses espérances...? Là où le dessin est énigmatique et nécessite une convention d'interprétation, la photo ne devrait pas l'être moins à ceci qu'elle participe d'une autre culture, celle de la magie claire de l'exactitude exécutée instantanément dans une inscription irréversible. Cette «prise de réalité» est insupportable, fascinante et difficile à maîtriser. Ici, Jean Nouvel a arraché quelques idées-images à sa propre réalité construite de façon à ce que l'on puisse mieux percevoir ce sur quoi se fonde sa conception de l'architecture. **Hubert Tonka**

A certain kind of architecture can only find in itself its own realities since the conception that carries it is not to refer to architectural art itself, but, precisely, to shape another one from all kinds of things that do not belong to it at first glance. If this architecture is an interrogation for the one who perceives it, it is an anxiety for the one who conceives it; for him it is a long wait. The edifice has to be achieved, received, then lived in. The experience of a new object does not work without requiring some adjustments. How can we experience an object with a new language? With old habits, or does it «naturally» form new ones? How can the sense encrusted in a space be felt where each one, like an electron upon silicon, creates his individual path, his momentary fragment of history in the fragile moment of the visit, of what we discover, of what we feel without perceiving consciously, finally all the brief moments which inscribe the memory of a scene, the passage into a brief instant of time of an uncertain form. Architecture is no longer deciphered as a redeeming theory, it imposes itself, rather, as a sequel, sometimes superimposed, of images. But the image as opposed to text does not know of any shared semiology, each develops a composite system, infinitely autonomous. The image production of a real object operates by the reduction of meaning, making another one appear. Thus the task of the designer of this architecture, more made out of interrogations than certainties, is to elaborate arguments from the very matter of architecture, for this reason, among other things, he pursues the meaning of his work in the photographic representations that will be divulged – it is less rare that he will not find it.

Jean Nouvel does not draw, he relates his visions in order to delay as much as possible the cruel instant where the concept becomes form, and crystallises into a figure. Does he need, today, to show in his way his crystallisations, to pursue his dreams and prolong his hopes...? Where the drawing is enigmatic and necessitates a convention of interpretation, the photo should not be less in the sense that it participates in another culture, that of the clear magic of instantly executed exactitude in an irreversible inscription. This «capture of reality» is unbearable, fascinating and difficult to master. Here, Jean Nouvel has pulled a few ideas-images out of his own constructed reality in order that we can better perceive what his conception of architecture is based on. **Hubert Tonka**

Die exakte Darstellung eines Willens

Sergio Cavero Heinrich von Kleist hat in seinem Aufsatz «Über die allmähliche Verfertigung der Gedanken beim Reden» geschrieben: «Wenn du etwas wissen willst und es durch Meditation nicht finden kannst, so rate ich dir, mein lieber, sinnreicher Freund, mit dem nächsten Bekannten, der dich aufstößt, darüber zu sprechen.» Erkennen Sie sich in diesem Zitat wieder? Welchen Gebrauch machen Sie beim Projektieren von der Diskussion und vom Wort? Welches sind die herausragenden Phasen und welches sind die Konsequenzen einer solchen Vorgehensweise?

Jean Nouvel Wenn man ein Projekt in Angriff nimmt, muß man immer erst alle guten Gründe suchen, weshalb es überhaupt durchgeführt werden soll. In diesem Sinn ist die Analyse die Vorbedingung für ein Projekt. Ich bin gegen jede architektonische Schöpfung, die auf einer Art unmittelbarer Intuition gründet, auf einem angeborenen Talent, das allein als Argument für ein Projekt und seinen Wert genügen soll. Zum Talent – meiner Ansicht nach bereits ein suspektes Wort – gehört auch immer ein starker Wille, und ein Projekt ist oft die exakte Darstellung eines Willens. Wo kein solcher Wille vorhanden ist, gibt es auch kein Projekt. Es ist deshalb sehr wichtig, sich alle Mittel zum Sehen und Wissen zu beschaffen. Sehen, weil man tatsächlich objektive und subjektive Dinge wahrnimmt, und wissen, weil es andere Aspekte gibt, die man nicht erkennen kann, wenn man sie nicht sucht – seien dies nun Aspekte der Geschichte, der Wirtschaft oder des menschlichen Umfelds. All diese Dinge sind nicht unmittelbar sichtbar. Wenn ich ein wichtiges Projekt in Angriff nehme, kümmere ich mich daher zuerst darum, möglichst viele Informationen zu sammeln. Das erinnert mich an Buckminster Fuller, der einmal gesagt hat: «Ich bin nicht besonders intelligent, aber ich bin gut informiert.» Wenn man gut informiert ist, gestaltet sich alles ein wenig einfacher. Das bedeutet zwar noch nicht, daß man sein Ziel auch erreicht, aber die Chancen dazu stehen ein bißchen besser. Bei bedeutenden Projekten oder bei Wettbewerben mit komplexen Programmen arbeite ich deshalb immer mit einem Analysten-

Team zusammen. Das tue ich natürlich nicht, wenn es sich um ein kleines, einfaches Projekt handelt, bei dem ich die näheren Umstände und Bedingungen der Situation bereits kenne. Dafür brauche ich kein zehnköpfiges Team.

Der andere Aspekt Ihrer Frage betrifft die Tatsache, daß die gesammelten Informationen selbstverständlich im Team diskutiert werden und wir Brainstorming-Sitzungen abhalten, aber egal wie unser Urteil auch ausfällt: es muß stets noch getestet werden. Dazu brauche ich meinen «Sparring-Partner», wie ich ihn nenne, den ich nach ganz bestimmten Kriterien auswähle: Es muß jemand sein, der eine andere Bildung hat als ich. In gewisser Hinsicht bin ich ein Vampir – ich sauge seine Bildung auf. Die Personen, die diese Rolle bisher gespielt haben, sind sehr exakt arbeitende Menschen: Jacques Le Marquet – ehemaliger Bühnenausstatter von Jean Vilar – ist Theaterautor und bringt deshalb eine auf das Theater ausgerichtete, szenografische, literarische und visuelle Bildung mit, die ich überhaupt nicht habe. Dann kam Olivier Boissière, Kunstkritiker, also Kritiker der bildenden Kunst und der Architektur: Er ist auch Schriftsteller und vertritt eine literarische Bildung, die ich ebenfalls nicht besessen habe und übrigens noch immer nicht besitze. Olivier Boissière hat seine Rolle als Sparring-Partner sieben oder acht Jahre lang gespielt. Jetzt ist es Hubert Tonka: Er hat eine philosophische Ausbildung genossen und arbeitet als Verleger, und auch er verfügt also über einen komplementären Blick und eine Bildung, auf die ich selber nicht automatisch zugreifen kann.

Im Grunde genommen treffen also stets zwei verschiedene kulturelle Sichtweisen aufeinander. Wenn ich eine Hypothese aufstelle, unterziehe ich sie gern diesem ersten Urteil, diesem ersten Filter, und oft komme ich dadurch auf eine Idee, an die ich vorher gar nicht gedacht hatte. Außerdem verläuft dieser Prozeß im freundschaftlichen Bereich, der auch äußerst dynamisch wirkt. Ich bin überzeugt, daß man gute Dinge nur mit Vergnügen schaffen kann; wenn man sich langweilt, ist das dem, was man produzieren will, bestimmt anzusehen. Wenn irgendwo eine optimistische Dimension – Wärme, Herzlichkeit – da ist, dann findet man sie auch wieder in dem, was man tut. Begeisterung ist nötig, und ich pflege diese Begeisterung, diese Lebenslust. Oft finden diese Brainstormings oder Sitzungen mit meinem Sparring-Partner am Tisch bei einer guten Flasche Wein statt, in einem nicht allzu schlechten Restaurant oder auch sehr spät abends.

Ein Projekt folgt zwangsläufig einem gewissen Ablauf, der es mit sich bringt, daß man während der Entwicklung hitzige Perioden durchlebt. Das heißt, daß man sich häufig sieht, miteinander telefoniert, weil einem etwas eingefallen ist, und sich im Büro trifft, wo das ganze Team anwesend ist. Der Druck steigt, es herrscht ein gewisser Optimismus, alle möglichen Hypothesen schwirren um den Tisch, und das einzige Problem besteht darin, sie dingfest zu machen. Es geht letztlich um eine Reihe von Aktionen, Zwischenfällen und Reaktionen, und ich glaube, dabei ist das Reden ganz besonders wichtig: verschiedene Hypothesen, Meinungen oder Urteile zu äußern. Im Grunde kommt es gar nicht so darauf an, was zuerst auf dem Tisch liegt: Wichtig ist, etwas dazu beizutragen und das Ganze dann zu gestalten. Auch aus etwas Dummem kann nach fünf, sechs Überlegungen oder auf Kritik hin etwas Interessantes entstehen. Das ist meine Methode – wobei ich mir eigentlich nicht sicher bin, ob sie so völlig eigenständig ist, aber auf jeden Fall entspricht sie meiner Persönlichkeit. Sie widerspiegelt meine Arbeitshaltung, und ich gelange auf diese Weise häufig zu unvorhersehbaren Ergebnissen.

Das ist ja letztlich das Interessante: das Unerwartete eines jeden Moments im Leben. Wenn es dieses Unerwartete nicht gäbe, wenn ich nicht wüßte, daß ich meine Meinung jeden Augenblick ändern könnte, wenn ich nicht wüßte, daß ich jeden Moment eine Information erhalten könnte, dank der ich mich weiterentwickeln kann, dann würde ich immer wieder das reproduzieren, was ich bereits seit vielen Jahren oder gar Jahrzehnten beherrsche. Und eigentlich wäre dies nichts anderes als eine narzißtische Übung oder der Ausdruck einer verknöcherten Persönlichkeit, die sich zwar vielleicht entwickelt, aber eben bloß in der Autarkie. Ich bin aber ganz gegen Autarkie, ich bin für Öffnung, für Offenheit, und daraus ergeben sich verschiedene Arbeitsmethoden. So versuche ich beispielsweise, Listen zusammenzustellen: alles, was man nicht tun soll, weil es idiotisch ist; alles, was man gern tun möchte, auch wenn es völlig unmöglich ist. Auf der einen Seite stehen dann die Wünsche, die unerreichten Sehnsüchte, und auf der andern Seite die Dinge, auf die man keinesfalls zurückgreifen sollte. Das ist zwar ein bißchen übertrieben, aber es hilft einem, eine Entscheidung zu fällen. Später wird dann manchmal alles wieder in Frage gestellt, und man sagt sich «Weshalb?». Und dieser Prozeß ist es, der schließlich zum Projekt hinführt.

*II
Die
exakte
Darstellung
eines Willens*

Man kann sich eine möglichst objektive Analyse, eine Art Sieb, nie ersparen. Es gilt, zuerst alles zu sehen, und dann müssen auf schöpferische Weise eine bestimmte Anzahl Hypothesen heranreifen. Ist dies einmal getan, sucht man natürlich nach Dingen, die einer möglichst vernünftigen Ordnung gehorchen. Als erstes wird eine Synthese aus all dem hergestellt, und diese zu produzieren, dieses Problem zu lösen ist viel schwieriger, wie Schachspielen. Später zeigt sich, daß nun zwar eine Grundlage vorhanden ist, das Wesentliche aber vielleicht noch fehlt. Auch das tritt also erst danach ein. Die Arbeit an einem Projekt ist langwierig, und es folgen sich mehrere Etappen; manche Dinge überlagern sich, widersprechen sich manchmal, und das Ganze verläuft alles andere als linear. Also reden wir schließlich über alles! Das erinnert mich übrigens an die Wohnungsfrage: Ich wollte mich von der Norm lösen, die in Frankreich in bezug auf den Wohnungsbau herrscht. Also habe ich mit Jean Le Marquet darüber gesprochen, und wir haben gewissermaßen eine erzählende Architektur geschaffen. Weil alles auf dem funktionalen Ansatz aufbaute, malten wir uns die schrecklichsten Geschichten aus: ein Mord in einer Wohnung, wie der Fluchtweg aussehen würde, falls jemand dort einbrechen wollte. Eine ganze Reihe Dinge, die im Grunde nichts mit der Funktionalität zu tun hatten, die aber dazu dienten, der Wohnung neben allem anderen eine menschliche Note zu geben, denn die objektive Materie an sich war völlig steril.

Der Architekt befindet sich in einer besonderen Lage, weil er selbst die Methode wählt, mit der er am weitesten kommt und das Projekt am besten vorantreiben kann. Als totalen Gegensatz dazu gibt es aber dieses ganze Hin und Her, all diese Diskussionen. Man muß sie zu ihrem Gegenteil parallel setzen und ausgleichen: Ruhe ist erforderlich, Konzentration ist erforderlich, und alle Argumente müssen noch einmal durchdacht werden. Sind einmal alle Analysen gemacht, alle Einwände angehört worden, muß ein Entscheid getroffen werden. Das nenne ich den kreativen Sprung. Obwohl ich also solange wie nur möglich gegen die Intuition ankämpfe, bedeutet das nicht, daß ich sie ganz ausschließe. Schließlich weiß ich sehr genau, daß ich an irgendeinem Punkt eine Lösung vorschlagen werde, die sich nicht nur aus der Analyse ergeben hat und die nicht allein das Resultat von Schlußfolgerungen ist. Im Gegensatz zu all diesem Hin und Her gibt es demnach einen ruhigen Moment: Normalerweise liege ich dabei im Bett und fange an nachzudenken. Ich brauche vielleicht zwanzig, fünfundzwanzig

Minuten volle Konzentration, und von da an laufen die Rädchen in meinem Kopf eine oder zwei Stunden lang wie geschmiert. Es gibt Beschleunigungen, ich verfalle ins Schwärmen, glaube, die Lösung gefunden zu haben, bin mir doch nicht ganz sicher, und schließlich sage ich: Das ist es. Ich muß wissen, daß die Stoppuhr läuft, ich muß wissen, daß morgen der letzte Termin für eine Entscheidung ist. Darin liegt zwar ein gewisses Risiko, aber es ist begrenzt, weil ich mich ja so lange wie möglich an möglichst handfeste Dinge gehalten habe. Ich bin in einem gewissen Sinne bereits kanalisiert; ich bin in all den Aspekten, die am meisten Sinn ergeben, bereits so weit gegangen, wie ich konnte.

Der kreative Sprung berührt meist das Problem der Formalisierung. Diesen Punkt finde ich sehr schwierig – und das ist vielleicht der Grund, weshalb Architekten in diesem Bereich nicht sehr gut sind –, denn man muß ständig gegen den Drang ankämpfen, allzu schnell zu formalisieren. Das bedeutet, daß ein formalistischer Architekt bereits weiß, welche Form entstehen wird, weil nur diese ihm gefällt und nur diese ihn interessiert. Mit demselben Anspruch wie ein Künstler im Bereich der bildenden Kunst hat man das Verlangen, sein Ding ganz weiß, ganz rund, genau dreieckig oder genau viereckig zu produzieren. Man will es so machen und weiß daher, daß man es letztlich auch tun wird. Dagegen versuche ich mich zu wehren – ich würde sogar sagen, daß ich ein nahezu masochistisches Vergnügen daran habe, diese offensichtlichste Wahl nicht zu treffen. Ich will die Form gar nicht kennen, solange ich nicht den ganzen Rest kenne. Dieser kreative Sprung stellt in Wirklichkeit zugleich die erste formale Entscheidung dar: Mit Rücksicht auf das, was ich über das Programm weiß, über das Gelände, über die kulturellen Gepflogenheiten, über die Wirtschaft, über all die Parameter halt, die eine Rolle spielen, entscheide ich mich für eine Formalisierung. Aber selbst wenn ich im Sinne einer Formalisierung von einer Form ausgehe, ist diese noch lange nicht unveränderlich. Ein Schritt ist getan, und man bewegt sich auf eine Form zu, diese wird sich jedoch noch glätten, noch verfeinern, und ganz allmählich wird sie auch facettenreicher werden. Ich bin übrigens nicht einer, der automatisch vom Allgemeinen zum Besonderen geht. Wenn man das Wesen von etwas erfaßt, sieht man oft, wo man anfangen kann, mit dem Wesen eines Innenraums zum Beispiel oder mit einer Einstellung auf einen bestimmten Teil.

Ein Schritt, der mich immer beschäftigt und der strategisch von großer Bedeutung ist, besteht darin, die Qualitäten einer bestimmten Lage zu erfassen. Ich habe das Institut du Monde Arabe an die Seite der Seine gestellt, obwohl ich gebeten wurde, es an die andere Seite zu plazieren, und ich wollte höher bauen, als dies das Reglement eigentlich erlaubte, denn nur so verfügt das Gebäude nun über einen Ausblick; der wäre sonst nicht möglich gewesen. Wenn ich Luzern aus einem bestimmten Winkel betrachte und alle Ecken freimache, dann geschieht dies, um einen Panoramablick sowohl auf die Stadt als auch auf den See zu erhalten: Dieser Blick fängt etwas ein, das im Grunde gar nicht existiert und nur schwer einzufangen ist. Man kann natürlich nicht sagen, daß es sich dabei um Architektur im eigentlichen Sinne handelt, weil ja keine Form an sich da ist; der Bau gewinnt dadurch aber eine Qualität hinzu. Wenn ich mich vor Luzern hinstelle und Postkarten-Ansichten ausschneide, dann deshalb, weil ich weiß, daß mir genau das gegeben ist und mit welchem Maßstab ich es zu tun habe. Ich versetze mich also in eine Lage, in der ich ein Gelände insgesamt oder eine Landschaft gleichsam erobern kann oder in der ich eine sinnvolle Beziehung dazu herstellen kann. All dies sind somit strategische Entscheidungen, die erst später zu Formen führen. Deshalb kann ich in Luzern nicht einen einzigen Pfeiler hinstellen. Wenn ich in dieses Panorama einen einzigen Pfeiler hinstellen würde, dann stände ich wie ein Trottel da ... Das Wunderbare ist ja, wie man den Blick von den Bergen bis zur alten Brücke schweifen lassen kann. Das ist nirgendwo sonst in Luzern so. Wenn mir das gelingt, dann ist mir bereits von der Strategie her ein außergewöhnlicher Bau gelungen. Alle Entscheidungen, die nach dieser ersten Bestandsaufnahme des Projekts gefällt werden, sind strategische Entscheidungen, aber es gibt auch formale Entscheidungen, die sich aufgrund eines Innenraums ergeben können oder die von einem bestimmten Geist eines Ortes abhängen, der mich beeindruckt hat und den ich extrapolieren will, oder aber auch ganz im Gegenteil durch die allgemeine Volumetrie im Verhältnis zum Rest.

Ich glaube sehr stark an einen fraktalen Ansatz, was bedeutet, daß es in der Architektur – vor allem in den letzten Jahren – nichts Unsinnigeres geben kann als die Vorstellung des vergrößerten Modells. Obwohl es einigen sehr gut gelingt, ist ein Modell, das einfach vergrößert wird, etwas Grauenhaftes, denn es löst keinerlei Gefühl in bezug auf Distanz, Kontaktaufnahme oder Einzelheiten aus. Ich liebe die Brüche im Maßstab, die ein fraktaler Ansatz ergibt. Sie führen dazu, daß man von einer Welt in eine andere übertritt, von einem ästhetischen oder sonst einem Gefühl zu einem andern. Indem ich den Geist des Projekts wahre, der eben in dieser Beziehung zwischen den verschiedenen Ebenen liegt, entdecke ich Dinge, die nichts miteinander zu tun haben. Wenn ich Sie beispielsweise von oben betrachte, dann sehe ich erst einen schönen schwarzen Kopf. Wenn ich näherkomme, dann sehe ich oben eine Brille, und noch näher erkenne ich Haare, die aus den Poren wachsen. Wenn ich dann eintrete, sind es Zellen: Immer ist es etwas anderes. Aber die Ansichten fallen primär gar nicht in Betracht, denn wenn ich ein Bild vergrößere, ist es nicht mehr dasselbe, weil ich jedes Mal ein neues und ganz andersartiges formales und emotionales Register entdecke. Um noch einmal auf das Beispiel Luzern zurückzukommen: Die große Platte von oben lesen ist das eine, aber von der Brücke aus eine Linie und einen Winkel zu lesen, das ist etwas anderes, und wenn ich unter der Auskragung sehe, wie die Fenster von allen Seiten zusammenkommen, dann ist das nochmals etwas anderes. Jedesmal trete ich von einer Welt in eine andere über, je nach Verschiebung und Annäherung des Blickwinkels. Sind durch dieses strategische Vorgehen einmal alle Elemente der Analyse vorhanden, erarbeite ich als erstes einige formale Aspekte. Innerhalb dieser formalen Aspekte beziehungsweise dieser formalen Strategie entwickle ich dann verschiedene Projekte innerhalb eines Projekts oder Empfindungen innerhalb von Empfindungen, immer abhängig vom Gesichtspunkt, der einmal weit entfernt ist und sich dann nähert, der einmal innen ist und dann wieder draußen … All diese möglichen Sichtweisen eines Projekts charakterisieren eine sogenannte konzeptionelle Architektur. Man könnte sie auch anders nennen, aber ihre Bedeutung ist die: Nur durch Verstand und eine völlig durchdachte Strategie gelingt es, auf überzeugende Weise ein Ziel zu erreichen.

Ich bin begeistert, wenn ein Projekt gleichzeitig 10'000 Projekte umfassen kann. Ein Projekt kann einheitlich sein und trotzdem eine derartige Komplexität aufweisen. Die Moderne wollte, daß ein Objekt lesbar, beschreibbar ist, daß alles auf Reinheit gründet, daß es nichts anderes gibt. Heute läßt sich sehr gut mit einer konzeptionellen Einheit spielen, mit einer Idee, die wie ein roter Faden durch das ganze Projekt verläuft. Je weiter man in einem Projekt aber vorankommt, desto mehr Dinge entdeckt man, die sich verstärken. Es ist die Lust am Entdecken, es ist die Lust, den Blick auf etwas Unerwartetes zu richten. Ich spreche hier aber nicht über etwas, das zwangsläufig auf einer klaren Diskontinuität oder Heterogenität aufbaut. Ich meine etwas, das genügend Tiefe besitzt, daß man es auf verschiedene Arten betrachten kann. Schließlich – und das ist ebenfalls eine alte Debatte – glaube ich, daß ein Kunstwerk eben genau das ist, was sich den Blicken nicht völlig preisgibt. Ein Kunstwerk ist demnach tot, sobald es kein Mysterium mehr in sich birgt. Ein Kunstwerk muß in der Lage sein, alle möglichen Menschentypen anzurühren, die sich dafür interessieren – unabhängig von ihrer Ausrichtung oder ihrer kulturellen Bildung. Die großen Meisterwerke der Literatur oder der Malerei sind allen zugänglich, wenn auch nicht auf dieselbe Weise. «Die Kartause von Parma» kann man als einfache Liebesgeschichte verstehen, als Annäherung an Italien oder als eine metaphysische Geschichte – sie läßt sich auf verschiedene Arten lesen. Bei großen Werken der Malerei ist das ähnlich. Die kleinste Einzelheit, etwa eine Hand, besitzt aufgrund der Art und Weise, wie sie gemalt ist, einen bestimmten Ausdruck. Ohne das ganze Gemälde gesehen zu haben, erkennen Sie bereits, ob es sich um ein gutes Werk handelt, und Sie wissen, daß Sie auf dem Bild zahlreiche Details sehen können. In der Architektur ist es ebenso: Es geht grundsätzlich um das Problem des Widerstands. Ich erinnere mich an eine Diskussion mit Jacques Le Marquet, in der er mich immer wieder fragte: «Wie tief muß man einen Schatz vergraben, um sicher zu sein, daß er entdeckt wird?» Gewiß, er muß entdeckt werden, aber eben nicht ganz …

Ich sage oft, ein Architekt sei gewissermaßen ein Verstärker. Jemand, der Gefühle oder Empfindungen einfängt und sich fragt: «Was kann ich daraus machen?» Sobald dieses Gefühl einmal für mich selbst genügend stark ist, fixiere ich mich darauf und verstärke es, damit niemand mehr daran vorbeikommt. Wenn es mich interessiert, kann ich alle Welt zum Hinschauen zwingen. Und wenn alle Welt hinschaut, dann wird es alle Welt schön finden müssen, denn mich hat es berührt, ich war bewegt. Es wird aber auch viele Leute geben, die das völlig uninteressant finden. Ich besitze deshalb nicht den Ehrgeiz, einen kulturellen Konsens zu schaffen – man kann sich nicht zum Ziel setzen, aller Welt zu gefallen. Ein architektonisches Werk bedeutet, ebenso wie ein Kunstwerk, ein Engagement, aber die verschiedenen Botschaften oder die verschiedenen Empfindungen, die man programmiert, müssen ihr Ziel schließlich auch erreichen. Im wesentlichen müssen sie lesbar sein – und wenn ich sage, lesbar, meine ich nicht, daß sie so groß wie das hier draufgeschrieben sind –, ich meine, daß sie faßbar sind. Von diesem Zeitpunkt an beginnt ein Gebäude sein eigenes Leben zu leben. Sobald man ein paar empfindliche Elemente gefunden hat, die ein wenig neu sind, kann man ziemlich sicher damit rechnen, daß einige Leute schockiert sein werden, denn es gibt eine Konvention der Empfindung, eine Konvention der Kunst, und wenn man sich nicht daran hält, kann man einigermaßen sicher sein, daß sich Widerstand regen wird. Im Gegensatz zu dem, was die Leute glauben, suchen wir diesen Widerstand aber nicht; wir versuchen nicht, das Bürgertum zu schockieren. Aber wenn diese Elemente für den Urheber einer Wahrheit entsprechen, und noch mehr, wenn sie zugleich der Gegebenheit einer Epoche entsprechen oder Dingen, die die ganze Welt bemerkt, dann ist es ganz einfach wahrscheinlich, daß das, was uns berührt, auch andere berührt. Solche Entscheidungen werden also aus diesen Gründen gefällt und keineswegs, um einen kulturellen Konsens zu finden, der ein lahmer Konsens wäre. Es ist bekannt, daß jede Schöpfung – im eigentlichen Sinn des Wortes – in ihrer ersten Phase eine Aggression ist und daß man das Vertrauen des Betrachters nur langsam und wahrscheinlich nicht auf einmal gewinnen kann. So wird dieser Ausgangspunkt allmählich immer mehr zulässig. Die Konvention des Schönen ist eine schreckliche Frage: Als Wim Wenders – den ich bekanntlich sehr gerne mag – anfing, Straßenbelag, Stromkabel und ähnliche Dinge als solche zu betrachten, lag darin eine Poesie, die den Vorübergehenden in den meisten Fällen nicht zugänglich war. Man mußte sie in die Ferne rücken, damit man am Ende bemerkte, was sich in ihnen verbirgt. Diese Poesie des Alltäglichen, der Dinge vor unseren Augen, hat sich uns nicht eingeprägt, sie hat uns nicht erreicht; all das war für uns nicht zu erkennen. Man muß deshalb immer Distanz schaffen, Distanz, dank der wir etwas auf eine andere Art sehen und dadurch dessen Schönheit erkennen können. Übrigens, um das wirklich dauerhafteste Gebäude zu schaffen – und das ist das einzig Dauerhafte in der Architektur –, muß dieses angemessen sein und vor allem muß es geliebt werden. Man glaubt immer, ein Gebäude müsse, um dauerhaft zu sein, aus Granit oder Beton errichtet werden, dabei ist das Gegenteil der Fall: Es muß so gebaut werden, daß es sehr schnell zum Symbol einer Haltung in einer bestimmten Epoche wird – denn dann wird es von allen gehätschelt. Deshalb sind die ersten zwanzig, dreißig Jahre für ein Bauwerk die schwierigsten; dann wird ihm noch kein Respekt entgegengebracht. Aber wenn man einmal zu verstehen beginnt, was es in bezug auf etwas ein wenig Seltsames, ein wenig

Knappes – ein wenig Geziertes – ausdrücken will, dann ist es, wie baufällig es auch sein mag, für eine gewisse Zeit aus dem Schneider.

Oft wird gesagt, daß ich mit Worten arbeite, und das stimmt auch. Aber Worte, was heißt das schon? Das sind ganz einfach Gedanken. Wenn man spricht, dann spricht man in einer Sprache, und Sprache ist für die Kommunikation und für den Austausch da: um einen Formalisierungprozeß zu beschleunigen und zu präzisieren. Leute, die entscheiden, bevor sie wissen, was eigentlich ihre Aufgabe ist, waren mir nie geheuer. Das war mein größtes Problem an der Ecole des Beaux-Arts. Ich habe gegen das angekämpft, was ich als «Kritzel-Intuition» bezeichne: Ständig folgt man seinem Bleistift, kritzelt irgendwas hin, dann noch etwas und noch etwas, und schließlich erliegt man der zwangsläufigen Nachsicht, die man sich selbst gegenüber übt. Sobald man drei schöne Linien fertiggebracht hat, sagt man: «So, das hätten wir, das war einfach und ist doch sehr schön herausgekommen.» ... Ich mißtraue jeder Formalisierung, die übereilt ist, jeder Formalisierung, hinter der nicht ein echter Wille steht, auf das heftigste. In diesem Sinn lehne ich die Intuition ab, ob diese nun im Kopf abläuft oder, was noch gefährlicher ist, sich durch eine Formalisierung ausdrückt – so könnte ich ja genauso gut aus dem Kaffeesatz lesen. Ich habe an der Ecole des Beaux-Arts unzählige Projekte gesehen, wahre grafische Wunderwerke waren das, die aber, in die Wirklichkeit umgesetzt, nichts an sich hatten, das ihnen Kraft verliehen hätte. Es besteht ein Riesenunterschied zwischen einer grafischen Kultur und einer architektonischen Kultur, zwischen dem Niederschreiben einer Partitur und der Musik, die durch die Interpretation dieser Partitur schließlich zu hören ist. An diesem Punkt ist das, was man Worte nennt, wichtig: Mit ihrer Hilfe versuche ich jegliche Selbsttäuschung zu vermeiden; Worte sind da, um Fallen ausfindig zu machen. Allerdings bin ich nicht absolutistisch: Ist eine Skizze erforderlich, um sich verständlich zu machen, dann fertige ich eben eine Skizze an. Gelangt man dann aber wieder in den Bereich der Formalisierung, müssen alle Dinge an ihrem Platz sein, und die Zeichnung darf nicht bremsen, sie darf kein Problem darstellen; sie muß enthemmend wirken, muß ein einfaches Mittel sein, das man völlig beherrscht. Ich weiß im übrigen immer, daß ich mein Projekt noch nicht zu Ende durchgedacht habe, wenn ich etwas über die Zeichnung suchen muß. Ich sage das den Architekten hier oft: Wenn man eine Fassade sucht, dann funktioniert etwas nicht. Man braucht eine Fassade nie zu suchen. Entweder ist etwas da, oder es ist nicht da; wenn man eine Fassade suchen muß, bedeutet dies, daß man nichts zu sagen hat, daß kein Programm vorhanden ist – ich meine hier das Programm, nach dem man zeichnet – und das bedeutet, daß auch keine Quelle fließt. Man jagt sich mit einer Zeichnung oft regelrecht Angst ein. Ich erinnere mich, als ich mir zum ersten Mal die Pläne für die Fondation Cartier anschaute und sogar beim Plan für die Südfassade des Institut du Monde Arabe, mit diesem extrem dichten Raster, da sagten die Leute beim Vorübergehen: «Der Ärmste, das funktioniert doch gar nicht ...!» Es ist zum Verzweifeln, wenn man einem Architekten der Bâtiments de France auf diese Weise seinen Gedanken erklären muß: Da herrscht ständig ein Unbehagen. Es ist natürlich nicht der Raster, der zählt, sondern das, was man darin oder durch ihn hindurch sehen wird; das, was programmiert ist oder eben nicht. Aber eine Zeichnung vermag eben oft nur ein Viertel dessen auszudrücken, was sie umfaßt. Sie ist zwar ein Instrument, um etwas darzustellen und herzustellen, aber sie muß eine Idee darstellen. Oft geht es gar nicht ohne Begleittexte. Außerdem gibt es Dinge, die sich eher für eine Zeichnung eignen als andere: Je elementarer etwas ist, desto besser läßt es sich mittels einer Zeichnung symbolisieren. Dies trifft etwa auf eine bestimmte klassische, opake Bauweise zu, die auf Volumen aufbaut, auf Schatten und Licht im Sinn einer Masse, auf projizierte Schatten, auf Eigenschatten und so weiter. Aber wenn man mit Begriffen wie Tiefe, Spiegelung, Architekturvariationen mit Licht, mit der Zeit, mit den Jahreszeiten arbeitet, dann genügt das nicht mehr. Dann muß man ein ganzes System in Bewegung setzen, ein System, so schwerfällig, daß es rein wirtschaftlich nicht mehr zu lenken ist. Also arbeitet man anders.

Ich mißtraue allem, was erstarrt. Ich denke aber auch nach, indem ich schreibe – beim Schreiben kann ich einen Gedanken vertiefen –, und ich betrachte Texte zu einem Projekt häufig als ebenso wichtig wie Zeichnungen, wenn nicht gar als noch wichtiger. Auf alle Fälle sind sie ganz klar eine Ergänzung. Ich habe nun einen großen Teil meiner architektonischen Laufbahn als Preisrichter verbracht und bin enttäuscht, daß Texte nicht das geringste Gewicht haben. Wenn ich in einer Architektur-Jury sitze – und das macht mir oft zu schaffen –, kommt es mir manchmal so vor, als hätte ich es mit lauter Analphabeten zu tun: Sie weigern sich schlicht, etwas zu lesen, und konzentrieren sich ausschließlich auf die Pläne. Es stimmt schon, daß es sich meist nicht lohnt, etwas zu lesen – aber hin und wieder ist es eben doch wichtig. Ich sage oft, daß es bei den meisten Wettbewerben zugeht, als würde etwa eine Oper allein aufgrund der Partitur bewertet, und zwar von Leuten, die weder Noten lesen können, noch – wenn sie es denn könnten – die Musik beim Lesen zugleich hören und sie sich vorstellen können. Es kommt zu einer Verzerrung: Wenn man sich beispielsweise bei einem Plan nicht auf etwas so Einfaches wie einen Maßstab beziehen kann und daher nicht weiß, was 15 oder 25 Meter Höhe bedeuten, dann versteht man überhaupt nichts mehr und ist also gar nicht in der Lage, sich in die Situation hineinzuversetzen. Ich glaube, das Geschriebene ist in diesen Dingen als Ergänzung wichtig; fast alles bedarf ständig einer Erklärung. Nun ist diese Erklärung aber erst dann besonders von Belang, wenn man etwas beweisen muß – und das Drama der Architekten besteht meiner Meinung nach darin, daß sie ständig etwas beweisen müssen. Es herrscht gewissermaßen ein institutionalisiertes Mißtrauen. Es sieht so aus, als wollten alle verstehen – aber wenn das bloß wahr wäre: Wenn doch nur alle Welt verstehen wollte und sich wirklich die Mittel dazu beschaffen würde, um sich bewußt zu werden, was auf dem Spiel steht! Tatsächlich ist es bei Wettbewerben so, daß die Erklärungen der Bauherrschaft oft nicht mehr als einen ersten Eindruck von einer Sache liefern und diese ihrerseits oft zu komplex ist, als daß man sie in ein paar Sekunden oder Minuten verstehen könnte. Und von einem gewissen Zeitpunkt an kann dann angesichts eines noch nicht realisierten Projekts wirklich nur noch etwas Schriftliches eine gewisse Anzahl von Intentionen überhaupt wieder einigermaßen ins Bewußtsein rücken.

Das Problem beim geschriebenen Text besteht darin, daß er keinen Beweis darstellt und daß die Architekten uns an großspurige Erklärungen gewöhnt haben, die meist überaus wortreich und ungenau sind. Ich will damit sagen, daß ein Architekt immer der Lüge verdächtigt wird. Und schon deshalb sollte man in die Lektüre der Texte eine gewisse Objektivität einfließen lassen. Es genügt nicht, einfach etwas zu sagen – man muß auch abklären, ob das Gesagte mit dem, was da ist, übereinstimmt. Man darf sich nicht von der – möglicherweise berechtigten – Begeisterung jedes Architekten täuschen lassen. Das Geschriebene besitzt, ebenso wie eine Zeichnung, eine Objektivität. Einige Dinge sind da, andere nicht. Man kann nicht einfach irgend etwas sagen. Eigentlich sollten alle bestraft werden, die einfach irgendwas sagen. Die meisten Wettbewerbe in Frankreich sind keine Wettbewerbe mit einer Jury auf kuturellem Niveau. Darin sitzen vielmehr Leute, die entweder zu genau wissen, was sie wollen, oder überhaupt nicht verstehen, was man ihnen erklärt, oder aber große Angst vor allem haben, was man ihnen sagt. Einen Wettbewerb kann man deshalb nur unter der Voraussetzung gewinnen, daß es sich um einen Architekturwettbewerb handelt, in dem über Architektur geredet wird. Die einzigen Wettbewerbe, die ich gewinnen konnte, waren solche, bei denen die Fragestellungen kultureller Natur waren. Bei der Präsentation für die Tour Sans Fins beispielsweise lastete eine derart große Spannung auf dem Projekt, und wir haben soviel daran gearbeitet, daß uns das alles ganz natürlich vorkam. Ich war dann aber sehr überrascht, als ich die Transkription von François Chaslin las. Was mich daran so verblüffte, war die Tatsache, daß sie wirkte wie ein konstruierter, schriftlich formulierter Text, was es doch gar nicht war. Ein wichtiger Punkt ist auch, daß das Ungesagte zweifellos in den Aufbau und in die Aussage des Textes mit einfließt. Das trifft im übrigen ebenso auf die Zeichnung zu wie auf den Text, die Gedanken und folglich auch auf die Architektur. Man braucht nicht alles zu sagen; gewisse Dinge verstehen sich von selbst und andere sind Folgen, die sich an zweiter und dritter Stelle ergeben.

Ich glaube zudem, daß noch etwas anderes mitspielt, nämlich daß man sich gewissermaßen selbst konstruiert: 300 oder 400 Projekte, das hinterläßt zwangsläufig Spuren. Folglich ergibt sich eine Art, die Dinge aufzufassen, eine gewisse Art, darüber nachzudenken, Abkürzungen vorzunehmen, und es entstehen bestimmte Ansichten. Wenn sich Michelangelo gegen Ende seines Lebens an einem Marmorblock zu schaffen machte, konnte man ziemlich sicher sein, daß dabei etwas Außergewöhnliches herauskommen würde. Das hing aber nicht mit dem Marmorblock zusammen, sondern mit der Tatsache, daß er sich selbst gewissermaßen bildhauerisch geformt hatte und weil er zudem ein guter Bildhauer war. Das gleiche gilt für einen Architekten, und so ist auch die alte Weisheit zu verstehen, daß ein Maler sein ganzes Leben damit verbringt, ein einziges Gemälde zu produzieren. Das trifft übrigens auf einen Maler eher zu als auf einen Architekten, weil ein Maler in seinen Obsessionen lebt, während ein Architekt immer durch das Äußere stimuliert wird. Trotzdem besteht aber zweifellos eine übereinstimmende innere Haltung, dank der sich in gewissem Sinne stets sagen läßt, daß alle Projekte in eine bestimmte Kategorie gehören oder daß es sich im Grunde um ein einziges Projekt handelt, das unter hundert verschiedenen Blickwinkeln betrachtet wird. Es gelingt nicht immer, sich vollständig von sich selbst zu lösen – man bleibt stets ein wenig in dem gefangen, was man bereits getan hat und in der Art, wie man es getan – oder eben als Architekt architektonisch geformt – hat.

Deshalb brauche ich einen «Sparring-Partner»: Er hilft mir manchmal, ein wenig weiter zu gehen, einen anderen Weg einzuschlagen. Und das ist eine echte Auseinandersetzung. Wenn ich für eine bestimmte Eigenart oder Hypereigenart eintrete, ist das keine Schrulle, sondern die Folge einer bestimmten Denkweise. Beim Anblick der meisten Bauwerke, die auf kulturbedingten Modellen beruhen und nichts mit der Umgebung zu tun haben, in der sie erstellt worden sind, frage ich mich unwillkürlich, was das im Grunde bedeutet. In diesem Bereich hat sich viel verändert: Wäre ich im 18. Jahrhundert Architekt gewesen, hätte ich mir mein Urteil wahrscheinlich anhand einer autonomen Disziplin gebildet, aufgrund voll und ganz anerkannter kulturbedingter Modelle, augrund von Typologien, die durchweg sinnvoll waren. Es gab ja auch keinen Grund, davon abzuweichen. Heute, da die Städte explosionsartig wachsen, erfordert jede Situation eine eigene Diagnose. Ohne eine solche Diagnose werden absurde Entscheidungen getroffen. Natürlich kann man diese Absurdität bewußt noch verstärken; man kann ein wenig boshaft sein; man kann sogar einer völlig primitiven und undenkbaren Stelle ganz automatisch Schönheit abgewinnen. Aber ich muß etwas aus den vorangegangenen Jahrhunderten bewahren: Obwohl ich nicht in Begriffen der Kontinuität denke und keineswegs glaube, daß die urbanen Formen noch die gleichen sind, bin ich doch überzeugt, daß man in bezug auf eine schon bestehende Situation immer noch etwas weiterentwickeln kann, das in einen Dialog hineinpaßt, das zum Wesen des Ortes gehört, zu seinem Akzent, und das ein wenig poetischer ist. Und wenn es einem gelingt, so etwas fertigzubringen, dann betrachte ich dies bereits als Daseinsberechtigung. Sonst würde ich mich wahrscheinlich mit etwas anderem beschäftigen. Ich glaube an zwei Grundsätze: Erstens ist es sinnlos, etwas zu bauen, woran man nicht glaubt, nur damit etwas gebaut wird. Es gibt viele Architekten, die nichts mit dieser Philosophie anfangen können; ihrer Meinung nach ist Bauen an sich sehr wichtig. Das ist eine sehr pragmatische Haltung; man muß schließlich auch leben. Aber wenn «leben müssen» der einzige Grund ist, dann soll man von etwas anderem leben. Das zweite Gebot besagt, daß ich alle Vorkehrungen treffen muß, um an diese Grenze zwischen Möglichem und Unmöglichem zu gelangen. Das ist, als würde ich auf den

Rand eines Abgrunds zugehen und sehen, wie dieser immer näherkommt; ich renne darauf zu, dann werde ich immer langsamer, bis ich mit einem Fuß im Leeren stehe und ... ich brauche nicht mit beiden ins Leere zu treten. Oft tue ich es allerdings. Wenn eine Sache historisch gesehen richtig ist, befindet sie sich genau auf dieser Linie, die entscheidet, ob etwas möglich wird, obwohl es unwahrscheinlich bleibt. Eine höchst unsichere Sache möglich machen – in diesem Bereich wird der architektonische Akt erregend.

Eine Zeitlang glaubte ich, diese Haltung werde allmählich immer stärker in den Zeitgeist eingehen und ich sei mit meinem Standpunkt zeitlich nur ein bißchen verschoben. Mittlerweile befürchte ich, daß diese Verschiebung groß ist, und ich weiß nicht, ob das ein gutes Zeichen ist, denn ich bin nicht sicher, ob es bedeutet, seiner Zeit voraus zu sein oder schlicht nicht zu wissen, was die Uhr geschlagen hat. Wer aber nicht pünktlich ist, verpfuscht ganz einfach eine Menge Dinge. In unserem Beruf müssen wir Ideen durchsetzen. Ein Architekt ist ein Vermittler, einer, der einen Schlüssel besitzt, um vom Virtuellen zum Realen zu gelangen, um einen Traum in die Wirklichkeit umzusetzen. Und dieser Umsetzungsprozeß ist interessant. Wenn aber der zeitliche Unterschied zwischen mir und denen, die mir zuhören und die mich beurteilen, zu groß ist, gelingt dies in neun von zehn Fällen nicht. Und das liegt nicht etwa an der Sprache, die ist kein echtes Hindernis. Ich sehe das bei meinen japanischen Freunden: Mit der Übersetzung klappt es immer, aber entscheidend ist in diesem Moment ganz besonders, daß Lust und Spaß an der Kommunikation da sind; wir können trotzdem miteinander lachen, aber das Tempo ist anders, es stellt sich nicht sofort ein gemeinsames Einverständnis ein. Deshalb ist noch viel mehr Willen oder meinetwegen Lust erforderlich, um einander zu verstehen. Aber seit ich meine Weltanschauung an Besonderheiten und Eigentümlichkeiten ausrichte, habe ich da keine Probleme mehr. Ich erwarte nicht, daß die Bedingungen in der Schweiz gleich sind wie in Frankreich, das würde mich im Gegenteil sehr enttäuschen. Ich liebe Unterschiede, damit habe ich echt keine Probleme. Ich würde sogar sagen, je mehr man mich drängt, eine Sache auf eine bestimmte Weise zu tun, die nicht spontan die meine ist, desto mehr interessiert mich das. Je nach Land sind die Reaktionen denn auch sehr verschieden. Manchmal trifft man auf Schwierigkeiten, auf Dinge, die man nicht so gut versteht; manchmal geht man vielleicht etwas weniger weit. Auf jeden Fall bin ich überzeugt, daß eine starke Architektur ohne eine Begegnung von Auftraggeber und Architekt nicht möglich ist. Das heißt, der Architekt allein genügt nicht, hat noch nie genügt ... Ein Auftraggeber allein übrigens auch nicht. Und dabei geht es nicht um die finanzielle Frage, sondern vielmehr um die Frage der Übereinstimmung. Wenn die Person, für die ich arbeite, nichts von meiner Arbeit versteht oder alles in Frage stellt, was ich tue, dann ist alles begrenzt, alles ist zerstört, alles ist verzerrt. Deshalb bin ich jedesmal, wenn ein Bau gelingt, der Person sehr dankbar, die ihn mit mir gemacht hat, und ich rede jetzt nicht von meinem Team, sondern von Auftraggebern: In Luzern würde es ohne Thomas Held kein Kultur- und Kongreßzentrum geben. Er hat die Bauherrschaft sensibilisiert und dadurch alles erst ermöglicht. Dazu waren ein eiserner Wille, Einfühlungsvermögen, ein Gemeinschaftsgefühl, Vertrauen nötig – ohne all das geht es nicht. Bei einem solchen Projekt sind die menschlichen Beziehungen entscheidend. Um eine Parallele zum Kino zu ziehen: Dort funktioniert es ebenso. Eigentlich müßte es auch bei einem Bauwerk einen Vorspann geben. Brigitte Metra, meine Assistentin in Luzern, hat dieses Projekt während langer Zeit vorangetrieben und mit ihr viele andere; auch Unternehmen haben sich begeistert dafür eingesetzt. Bei einem so großen Projekt ist es also eine ganze Abfolge von Willenskräften – von Leidenschaften –, mit denen auf ein Ziel hingearbeitet wird. Und es ist Aufgabe des Architekten, das Ziel möglich zu machen, aber das ist nicht immer evident ...

Sergio Cavero *Was halten Sie von der Idee, das Kultur- und Kongreßzentrum zu fotografieren, den Bau auf einen Filmstreifen zu bannen?*

Jean Nouvel Das ist letztlich eine völlig natürliche Sache, und deshalb habe ich es auch angeregt. Meiner Meinung nach gibt es eine Reihe konzeptioneller Intentionen, die man im nachhinein verifizieren oder durch Fotos belegen könnte. Möglich wären aber auch Fotos konzeptioneller Natur, welche die grundsätzlichen Dinge hervorheben und die ganz entschieden in die Richtung unseres doch eher fraktalen Ansatzes gehen. Das wäre dann nicht zwangsläufig die unmittelbare Ansicht, sondern es ginge vielmehr darum, verschiedene Maßstäbe, ein Gelände und einen Bau, miteinander in Verbindung zu setzen. Also, letztlich ist das wohl ein Mittel, die Zielsetzungen des Projekts aufzulisten, wieder neu aufzulisten und sie sichtbar zu machen...

Überarbeitete Fassung eines Gesprächs mit Jean Nouvel am 9. Juni 1998 in Paris, 10 cité d'Angoulême. Leitung des Gesprächs und Bearbeitung des Textes durch Sergio Cavero (Neuchâtel 22.9.1969, Architekt; ab 1994 Assistent Eidg. Technische Hochschulen in Zürich ETHZ und Lausanne EPFL, lebt und arbeitet in Zürich).

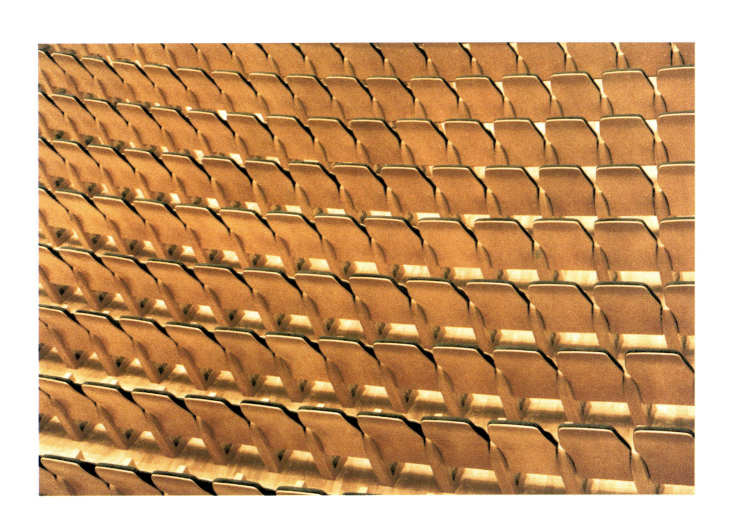

L'exacte représentation d'une volonté

Sergio Cavero Heinrich von Kleist écrit dans «De la constitution progressive des pensées dans le discours» : «*Si tu veux savoir quelque chose et que tu ne le trouves pas par la méditation, je te conseille, mon cher ami, d'en parler avec la prochaine connaissance que tu rencontreras*»[1]. Vous reconnaissez-vous dans cette réflexion ? Quel usage faites-vous de la discussion et de la parole dans votre processus de projet ? Quelles en sont les phases saillantes et quelles sont les conséquences de cette manière de procéder ?

Jean Nouvel À chaque fois que l'on commence un projet, il s'agit de débusquer toutes les bonnes raisons de le faire. Dans ce sens l'analyse est la condition du projet. Je suis en effet à l'opposé de toute création architecturale basée sur une sorte d'intuition créatrice immédiate, sur un talent inné qui permettrait de trouver seul, en soi-même, les raisons et les valeurs d'un projet. Le talent – qui est un mot suspect à mes yeux – c'est quand même toujours beaucoup de volonté, et le projet, c'est souvent l'exacte représentation d'une volonté. S'il n'y a pas cette volonté, il n'y a pas de projet. Je crois donc qu'il est très important de se donner avant tout les moyens de voir et de savoir. Voir, parce qu'effectivement on capte des choses objectives et subjectives, et savoir, parce qu'il y a d'autres choses qu'on ne peut pas savoir si on ne va pas les chercher, qu'elles soient de l'ordre de l'histoire, qu'elles soient de l'ordre de l'économique ou de l'humain. Toutes ces choses-là ne se voient pas immédiatement. Donc, quand je commence un projet important, je me mets dans les conditions de réunir un maximum d'informations. Cela me rappelle ce que disait Buckminster Fuller : «je ne suis pas très intelligent, mais je suis bien informé». Dès qu'on est bien informé, cela va déjà un tout petit peu mieux. Cela ne veut pas dire qu'on va y arriver, mais cela veut dire qu'on a un peu plus de chances d'y arriver. Sur des projets importants, sur des concours aux programmes

1. «Wenn du etwas wissen willst und es durch Meditation nicht finden kannst, so rate ich dir, mein lieber, sinnreicher Freund, mit dem nächsten Bekannten, der dich aufstösst, darüber zu sprechen. (...)», Heinrich von Kleist *in* Über die allmähliche Verfertigung der Gedanken beim Reden, 1805/06, (vol. 7, 2ᵉ édition, Kleist «Werke und Briefe», publ. par Erich Schmidt et Georg Minde-Pouet).

complexes, je constitue autour de moi une équipe d'analystes, sauf bien sûr s'il s'agit d'un petit projet très simple dont je vois les tenants et les aboutissants et pour lequel je ne vais pas constituer un groupe de dix personnes.

L'autre aspect de la question est que, quand les informations arrivent, certes, elles sont discutées en équipe, nous faisons des séances de *brainstorming*, mais, quelque soit le diagnostic qu'on est amené à faire, il faut le tester. C'est pourquoi j'ai toujours eu besoin de ce que j'appelle un *sparring-partner*, qui est quelqu'un que je choisis sur des critères très particuliers : il faut que ce soit quelqu'un qui ait une culture différente de la mienne. En quelque sorte, je suis un vampire ; je vampirise sa culture. Les gens, qui ont rempli ce rôle-là, sont des gens très précis : c'était Jacques Le Marquet – qui était le scénographe de Jean Vilar – qui est un auteur de théâtre et qui donc a une culture théâtrale, scénographique, littéraire, visuelle, que je n'ai absolument pas ; c'était Olivier Boissière qui est un critique d'art d'abord – d'arts plastiques et d'architecture – qui est aussi un écrivain et qui a une culture littéraire que je n'ai pas, que je n'avais pas et que je n'ai toujours pas d'ailleurs. Olivier Boissière a rempli son rôle auprès de moi pendant sept ou huit ans. Maintenant, c'est Hubert Tonka, qui lui a une formation de philosophe, qui est éditeur et qui a un regard une fois de plus complémentaire au mien et une culture que je n'ai pas automatiquement.

Donc, en fait, il y a confrontation de deux points de vue culturels : quand j'émets une hypothèse, j'aime la confronter à ce premier jugement, à ce premier filtre, et souvent cela me renvoie à une chose à laquelle je n'avais pas pensé. Et puis tout ceci se passe aussi sur le registre, lui aussi très porteur de dynamique, de l'amitié. Je crois qu'on ne fait des bonnes choses que dans le plaisir et que si l'on s'ennuie vraiment, cela se voit dans ce que l'on va produire. S'il y a une dimension optimiste en tout cela – une chaleur – cela se retrouve dans tout ce que l'on fait. Il faut de l'enthousiasme en fait, et je cultive cet enthousiasme, ce plaisir de vivre : souvent, ces *brainstormings* ou ces réunions avec mon *sparring-partner*, se passent autour de la table, avec une bonne bouteille entre nous, dans des restaurants qui ne sont pas trop mauvais ou tard dans la nuit.

Il a une sorte d'implication dans le projet, qui fait que, quand un projet se développe, on vit des périodes chaudes; c'est-à-dire qu'on se voit souvent, on se téléphone, parce qu'on vient de penser à quelque chose, on se retrouve à l'agence où il y a toute l'équipe. La pression monte, il y a une sorte d'optimisme et toutes les hypothèses fusent autour de la table, le seul problème étant de les arrêter au vol. Il s'agit finalement de toute une série d'actions, d'incidents, de réactions, et je crois qu'il est très important de parler, d'émettre un certain nombre d'hypothèses, d'avis ou de jugements. Au fond l'important n'est pas tellement ce que l'on met sur la table d'abord : ce qui compte, c'est d'y mettre quelque chose et puis ensuite de le façonner. Même si l'on dit une bêtise, il peut en naître quelque chose d'intéressant après cinq ou six réflexions, après cinq ou six critiques. Cette méthode-là est la mienne et je ne suis pas sûr qu'elle soit totalement originale, mais en tous les cas, elle correspond à mon personnage, elle correspond à ma philosophie d'un travail comme celui-là et elle débouche sur des choses souvent imprévisibles.

Finalement c'est cela qui est intéressant; c'est l'aventure de chaque instant dans une vie. S'il n'y a pas cette aventure, si je ne sais pas qu'à chaque moment je peux changer d'avis, si je ne sais pas qu'à chaque moment on peut m'apporter une information susceptible de me faire évoluer, je vais reproduire ce que je sais depuis déjà quelques années – ou quelques dizaines d'années – et au fond, cela sera un exercice de pur narcissisme ou l'expression d'une personnalité figée, qui évolue peut-être, mais en autarcie. Je suis donc contre l'autarcie, je suis pour cette ouverture et à partir de là naissent un certain nombre de méthodes. On essaie par exemple de faire des listes : tout ce qu'il ne faut pas faire, parce que c'est idiot; tout ce qu'on aimerait faire, même si c'est strictement impossible. D'un côté, il y a des souhaits, il y a des désirs absolus, et de l'autre les choses dans lesquelles il ne faut surtout pas rentrer. C'est un peu caricatural, mais cela aide à faire le tri, et puis quelquefois on remet tout en cause, on dit «pourquoi?» : c'est ce processus-là qui amène au projet.

On ne fait jamais l'économie d'une analyse la plus objective possible, d'une sorte de tamis; il faut d'abord tout voir et ensuite il faut évoquer de façon générique un certain nombre d'hypothèses. Une fois qu'on a fait cela, évidemment on recherche des choses qui sont d'un ordre plus sensible. On cherche d'abord la synthèse de tout cela qui, elle, est un problème beaucoup plus dur à résoudre, comme les échecs. Une fois qu'on a fait cela, on se rend compte qu'on tient une base, mais qu'en fait, peut-être, l'essentiel n'est pas encore là. Donc c'est après que cela se passe aussi : après on évoque ce genre de choses, et le travail sur un projet est un travail long, ce sont plusieurs étapes, ce sont des choses qui se superposent, qui se contredisent à un certain moment, ce n'est pas du tout linéaire. Donc finalement, on parle de tout ! Cela me rappelle ce qui s'est passé pour le logement : je voulais sortir de la norme du logement en France et j'en parlais avec Jacques Le Marquet et nous faisions pratiquement une architecture narrative. Parce que tout était basé sur l'approche fonctionnaliste, nous nous mettions à imaginer les pires histoires : un meurtre dans l'appartement, la façon dont on sortait de là si on voulait voler. Toute une série de choses qui n'avaient rien à voir avec la fonctionnalité, mais qui étaient une façon de remettre dans l'appartement un peu d'humanité à partir d'autres ingrédients, parce que la matière objective était castratrice.

L'architecte est dans une position très particulière parce que c'est lui-même qui organise la méthode qui va lui permettre d'arriver le plus loin, d'avancer le plus possible dans le projet. Mais en contraste avec cela il y a toute cette agitation, toutes ces discussions. Il faut les mettre en parallèle avec l'inverse : il faut le silence, il faut la concentration, il faut repasser dans sa tête tous les arguments. Une fois que toutes les analyses sont là, que tous les raisonnements ont été tenus, il faut choisir. C'est ce que j'appelle un saut créatif. Alors, même si je me bagarre contre l'intuition, le plus longtemps possible, cela ne veut pas dire que je la récuse totalement, puisque je sais bien qu'à un moment, je vais proposer quelque chose qui ne sera pas entièrement de l'ordre de l'analyse, qui ne sera pas entièrement le produit d'une déduction. Il y a donc un moment où, à l'opposé de cette agitation, je me retrouve en général dans mon lit et je commence ; j'ai besoin de vingt, vingt-cinq minutes de bonne concentration et à partir de là, durant une heure ou deux, la mécanique tourne très rond : il y a des accélérations, il y a des exaltations, je crois que j'ai trouvé, je ne suis pas sûr, et finalement je dis : voilà. Il faut que je sache que le chronomètre tourne, que je sache que le lendemain sera le dernier moment pour prendre une option. Il y a dans ceci quelque chose qui est de l'ordre du risque, mais pour moi, c'est un risque limité, en ce sens que je me suis tenu aux choses les plus solides le plus longtemps possible. Je suis en quelque sorte déjà canalisé : je suis déjà allé le plus loin que je pouvais dans les choses qui font le plus de sens.

Ce saut créatif touche le plus souvent au problème de la formalisation. Une chose qui est très difficile, je crois, – et c'est pour cela que peut-être tous les architectes ne jouent pas à ce sport-là – c'est qu'il faut contrer le désir permanent de formaliser vite. C'est-à-dire que si on est un architecte formaliste, on sait déjà quelle forme on va faire, parce qu'il n'y a que celle-là qui nous plaît, qui nous intéresse ; au même titre qu'un artiste dans le domaine des arts plastiques, on a envie de faire notre truc tout blanc, un truc tout rond, un truc tout triangulaire, un truc tout carré. On a envie de le faire, donc on sait qu'on va en arriver là. J'essaie de ne pas faire cela, et je dirais même que j'arrive à trouver un plaisir, peut-être un peu masochiste, à décaler ce choix le plus possible : je ne veux pas connaître la forme, tant que je ne sais pas tout le reste. Ce saut créatif est en fait le premier choix formel : compte tenu de ce que je sais du programme, du site, des habitudes culturelles, de l'économie, de tous les paramètres qui sont en jeu, je vais choisir une formalisation. Mais même quand je pars dans la forme, dans l'esprit d'une formalisation, elle n'est pas définie pour autant. On a fait un pas et on va vers quelque chose qui va se polir, va s'affiner, et petit à petit la forme va s'enrichir. Je ne suis d'ailleurs pas automatiquement quelqu'un qui va du global au particulier. Quand on prend l'esprit de quelque chose souvent on voit que l'on peut commencer par l'esprit d'un intérieur ou par un cadrage sur quelque chose, par exemple. Un point qui me questionne constamment et qui est stratégiquement très important, c'est le fait de conquérir les qualités d'une situation. Si j'ai placé l'Institut du Monde Arabe du coté de la Seine, alors qu'on m'incitait à le mettre de l'autre coté, et si je l'ai voulu plus haut que le règlement ne l'autorisait, c'est pour que ce bâtiment arrive à conquérir une vue qu'il n'aurait sinon jamais eue. Si je me mets à Lucerne sur l'angle et si je dégage tout l'angle, c'est pour avoir cette vue panoramique à la fois sur la ville et sur le lac qui conquiert quelque chose qui n'existe pas, et qui est difficile à conquérir. On ne peut pas dire que ceci soit de l'architecture au premier degré, car ce n'est pas la forme elle-même qui est là, c'est simplement que le bâtiment conquiert en plus cette qualité-là. Si je me mets en face de Lucerne et si je découpe des cartes postales, c'est parce que je sais que j'ai cela et que je sais quelle échelle j'ai en face, et donc je me mets en situation de conquérir ou de prendre un sens par rapport à un site général ou à un paysage. C'est tous ces éléments-là, qui deviennent donc des choix stratégiques et qui seulement alors conduisent à des formes. C'est pour cette raison que je ne peux pas avoir un seul poteau à Lucerne : si j'ai un poteau sur ce panoramique, j'ai l'air d'un con... Ce qui est magnifique, c'est ce travelling, de la montagne au vieux pont : il n'y pas un autre lieu de Lucerne qui possède cela. Donc, si j'offre cela, j'offre déjà une architecture exceptionnelle dans sa stratégie. Tous ces choix-là, qui se font à la suite de cette mise en charge du projet, sont des choix stratégiques, mais ce sont aussi des choix formels qui peuvent partir d'un intérieur, qui peuvent partir d'un esprit du détail par rapport à un lieu qui m'aura frappé dans la ville et que je vais extrapoler, mais qui peuvent aussi partir, à l'opposé, d'une volumétrie générale que je trouverai, en relation avec le reste.

Je crois beaucoup à l'approche fractale, c'est-à-dire qu'il n'y a rien de plus nul en architecture – surtout ces dernières années – que la notion de maquette agrandie. Bien que certains fassent cela très bien, une simple maquette agrandie est quelque chose d'épouvantable, parce qu'elle n'évoque aucune émotion en fonction de la distance, en fonction du toucher ou en fonction du détail. Ce que j'aime, c'est les ruptures d'échelle qu'il y a dans l'approche fractale, qui font qu'on passe d'un monde à un autre, d'une émotion esthétique, ou d'un registre, à un autre. Tout en gardant l'esprit du projet, qui va justement être cette relation entre ces différents plans, je découvrirai des choses qui n'ont rien à voir les unes avec les autres. Par exemple, si je vous regarde d'en haut, je vois une belle tête noire, si je m'approche, je vais commencer à voir des lunettes sur le dessus, puis si je m'approche, je vais voir des cheveux plantés dans des pores, puis si je rentre à l'intérieur, ce sera des cellules : ce sera toujours autre chose. Mais les vues n'entrent pas en ligne de compte : il ne s'agit pas de la même image qui est agrandie, car je vais découvrir à chaque fois un registre formel et émotionnel qui sera de nature très différente. Si l'on reprend l'exemple de Lucerne, le fait de lire d'en haut la grande plaque, c'est une chose, mais le fait de lire depuis le pont une ligne et un angle, c'est une autre chose, et si, sous le porte-à-faux, je vois tous les verres s'accumuler de chaque côté, c'est encore autre chose : à chaque fois, je passe d'un monde à un autre en fonction de ce déplacement et de cette proximité du regard. Ce que j'élabore une fois que tous les éléments d'analyse sont là, au travers d'une stratégie, c'est d'abord quelques aspects formels et c'est dans ces aspects formels ou dans cette stratégie formelle, que je développe par la suite des projets dans le projet, ou des sensations dans les sensations, en fonction d'une vue qui est lointaine, rapprochée, intérieure, extérieure, etc. Tous ces angles de vue dans le projet sont des choses qui caractérisent ce que j'appelle une architecture conceptuelle. On peut appeler ça autrement, mais cela veut dire qu'il n'y a que l'esprit et qu'une stratégie totalement pensée qui peuvent permettre d'aboutir à cela de façon convaincante.

En fait, je suis ravi si un projet peut en être dix mille simultanément. Il n'y a aucun rapport entre l'unité du projet et le fait qu'il ait cette complexité-là. L'époque moderne voulait qu'un objet soit lisible, décryptable, que tout soit basé sur la pureté, qu'il n'y ait plus rien après. Aujourd'hui, on peut très bien jouer sur une unité conceptuelle, sur une idée qui traverse tout le projet, mais au fur et à mesure qu'on avance dans le projet, on découvre beaucoup de choses qui se renforcent. C'est le plaisir de la découverte, c'est le plaisir de poser le regard sur une chose inattendue, mais je ne parle pas là d'une chose qui serait basée automatiquement sur la discontinuité affirmée ou sur l'hétérogénéité. Je parle de quelque chose qui a suffisamment de profondeur pour être vue de multiples façons différentes. Finalement – et c'est là un vieux débat aussi – je considère qu'une œuvre d'art, c'est justement ce qui résiste à tous les regards, c'est-à-dire que s'il n'y a pas de mystère, on peut dire que l'œuvre d'art est morte. Une œuvre d'art doit être capable de toucher à peu près tous les types de personnes qui s'intéressent à cela – quelque soit leur orientation ou leur niveau culturel : les grands chefs-d'œuvre de littérature ou de peinture sont accessibles à tous, bien que peut-être pas de la même façon : dans «La Chartreuse de Parme» vous pourriez voir une simple histoire d'amour, toute une approche sur l'Italie, toute une métaphysique, vous pourriez la lire à différents degrés. Quand on voit les grandes œuvres de peinture, c'est pareil; le moindre détail, une main par exemple, à la façon dont elle est peinte, à son expression, sans avoir vu tout le tableau, vous savez déjà que c'est une bonne peinture et vous savez que vous allez avoir dans le tableau de multiples choses à voir. En architecture, c'est assez semblable. Il s'agit fondamentalement d'un problème de résistance : je me souviens de cette discussion que j'avais avec Jacques Le Marquet, qui me disait toujours : «A quelle profondeur faut-il enfouir un trésor pour être sûr qu'il soit découvert ?» Oui, il faut qu'il soit découvert, mais pas entièrement...

Je dis souvent qu'un architecte, c'est un amplificateur, c'est quelqu'un qui va capter des émotions ou des sensations et qui se demande : «qu'est-ce que je peux faire de ça ?» Si finalement cette émotion a été assez forte pour moi, je vais me cristalliser dessus et je vais l'amplifier, pour que personne ne puisse passer à côté : si cela m'intéresse, je vais obliger tout le monde à regarder. Selon moi, si tout le monde regarde, tout le monde doit trouver cela beau, puisque cela m'a touché, puisque j'ai été ému, mais il y aura beaucoup de personnes qui trouveront cela absolument sans intérêt. Je n'ai donc aucune vocation au consensus culturel; on ne peut pas avoir la prétention de plaire à tout le monde. Une œuvre architecturale comme une œuvre d'art est un engagement, mais les différents messages ou les différentes sensations qu'on programme doivent toucher leur but. Pour l'essentiel elles doivent être lisibles – et quand je dis lisibles, cela ne veut pas dire écrit dessus gros comme cela – cela signifie qu'on les capte. À partir de là le bâtiment vit sa vie : à partir du moment où l'on a trouvé un certain nombre d'éléments sensitifs qui sont un peu neufs, on est à peu près sûr de choquer un certain nombre de personnes, parce qu'il y a une convention de la sensation, une convention de l'art et si l'on est à côté, on peut être à peu près certain qu'il y aura une résistance. Et contrairement à ce que les gens pensent, on ne la recherche pas cette résistance, on ne cherche pas à choquer le bourgeois. Simplement, si ces choses-là correspondent à une vérité de l'auteur et si elles correspondent en plus à une réalité par rapport à une époque ou à des choses que tout le monde perçoit, il y a peut-être une chance que ce qui nous touche, touche aussi les autres. Donc, ces choix sont faits sur la base de ces raisons-là et pas du tout pour aller vers ce consensus culturel qui est une sorte de consensus mou. On sait très bien que toute création – au sens réel du terme – dans un premier temps est une agression et que, seulement petit à petit, peut-être pas en une fois, il faut apprivoiser le visiteur ; ainsi ce point de départ devient peu à peu une chose qui est plus admise. La convention du beau est une terrible question : quand Wim Wenders – que j'aime beaucoup, tout le monde le sait – a commencé à regarder le macadam, les fils électriques et des choses comme cela, c'était une poésie qui était, la plupart du temps, inaccessible au passant ; il fallait qu'elle soit distanciée pour que l'on se rende compte finalement de ce qu'elle recelait. Cette poétique du quotidien, alors que les choses sont sous nos yeux, n'arrivait pas à nous imprimer, n'arrivait pas à nous atteindre, tout cela était transparent pour nous ; il faut donc toujours créer cette distance qui nous permet de regarder la chose d'une autre façon et de capter sa beauté. Je pense d'ailleurs que si l'on veut créer le bâtiment qui soit le plus permanent – et c'est la seule permanence qu'il y ait dans l'architecture –, il faut qu'il soit adéquat, et surtout qu'il soit aimé. On croit toujours que la façon de faire le bâtiment le plus pérenne, c'est de le faire en granit ou en béton ; au contraire, il faut faire en sorte que, très vite, il devienne le symbole d'une attitude par rapport à une époque : à partir de ce moment-là tout le monde le choie. C'est pour cela que souvent les années les plus difficiles pour un bâtiment sont les vingt ou trente premières, parce que, il n'y a pas encore de respect. Mais, dès qu'on commence à comprendre ce qu'il veut dire par rapport à une chose un peu rare, un peu précise – un peu précieuse –, à ce moment-là, aussi fragile soit-il, il est parti pour un certain temps.

On a souvent dit que je travaillais avec les mots, ce qui est vrai. Mais les mots qu'est-ce que cela veut dire ? Cela veut simplement dire la pensée. Si on parle, on parle une langue et la langue, c'est fait pour communiquer et pour échanger : pour accélérer et pour préciser un processus de formalisation. J'ai toujours eu horreur des gens qui décident avant de savoir ce qu'ils ont à faire. Cela a été mon premier problème à l'École nationale des beaux-arts, je me suis bagarré contre ce que j'appelais « l'intuition crayonnante » : on suit son crayon tout le temps, on fait un petit gribouillis, puis on en fait un autre et puis un autre, et puis finalement, on ressentira l'automatique indulgence qu'on a vis-à-vis de soi-même, c'est-à-dire que dès qu'on a fait trois beaux traits ensemble, on va dire : « ah, et bien voilà, c'était très simple et c'est très beau »... Je me méfie très fortement de tout ce qui est formalisation hâtive et formalisation qui n'est pas soutenue par une vraie volonté. Donc, c'est dans ce sens que je récuse une forme d'intuition, que cette intuition soit dans la tête ou, ce qui est encore plus dangereux, dès qu'elle se traduit par une formalisation, ce qui s'apparente finalement à lire dans le marc de café. J'ai tellement vu de projets à l'École nationale des beaux-arts qui étaient des splendeurs graphiques, mais où il n'y avait absolument rien qui était de nature, une fois qu'ils auraient passé dans le réel, à leur donner cette force-là. Il y a une énorme différence entre une culture graphique et une culture architecturale, entre écrire une partition et la musique que l'on va entendre, une fois qu'elle sera interprétée. C'est là que ce que l'on appelle les mots sont importants : grâce à eux, j'essaie de ne pas me faire abuser, les mots sont là pour détecter tous les pièges. Et ceci sans être absolutistes : quand il faut un croquis pour se faire comprendre, et bien, on fait un croquis. D'ailleurs dès qu'on rentre dans la phase de formalisation, toutes les choses doivent être en place et le dessin ne doit pas être un frein, il ne doit pas être un problème, il doit être désinhibé : il doit être un simple moyen, que l'on maîtrise complètement. Mais je sais qu'à chaque fois que je cherche quelque chose par le dessin, c'est que je ne suis pas au bout de mon projet. Je dis souvent aux architectes ici que quand on cherche une façade, c'est que quelque chose ne va pas. On n'a jamais à chercher une façade. Ou la chose est là, ou elle n'est pas là : dès qu'on cherche une façade, c'est qu'on n'a rien à dire, c'est que le programme n'est pas là – je parle du programme de ce que l'on dessine – et c'est que cela ne coule pas de source. On se fait souvent très peur par le dessin. Je me souviens de la première fois où j'ai vu les plans de la Fondation Cartier, ou même le plan de la façade sud de l'Institut du Monde Arabe, avec cette trame si dense : les gens qui passaient à côté de moi disaient : « Le pauvre, ce n'est quand même pas possible... ». C'est désespérant de devoir expliquer ainsi sa pensée à un architecte des Bâtiments de France : il y a toujours un malaise. Évidemment, ce qui est important ce n'est pas la trame, mais c'est ce qu'on va voir dedans, c'est ce qu'on va voir à travers, c'est ce qui est programmé ou pas. Mais le dessin souvent ne dit pas le quart de ce qu'il contient. C'est un outil pour représenter et pour produire, mais il doit représenter une idée. Souvent, il faut le compléter par des textes. D'ailleurs il y a des choses qui se prêtent plus au dessin que d'autres : plus la chose est primaire, plus elle peut se symboliser par un dessin. On peut dire cela d'une certaine architecture classique opaque, basée sur les volumes, sur l'ombre et la lumière au sens masse, ombre projetée, ombre propre, etc. Mais dès que l'on rentre dans des notions de profondeur, de reflets, de variations de l'architecture avec la lumière, avec le temps, avec les saisons, cela ne suffit plus. Il faut mettre en mouvement tout un système qui est tellement lourd qu'économiquement, il n'est plus absolument gérable. Donc on fonctionne autrement.

    Je me méfie de tout ce qui fige. Mais je réfléchis aussi par l'écrit – je peux approfondir une pensée par l'écrit – et je considère que sur les projets souvent les textes sont aussi importants ou plus importants que les dessins, ou en tout cas strictement complémentaires. Et ce qui me désole, après avoir passé une bonne partie de mon expérience architecturale dans les jurys, c'est que je me rends compte que les écrits n'ont absolument aucun poids. Quand je suis dans un jury d'architecture – souvent je me bagarre à cause de ça –, c'est à croire qu'on a affaire à des analphabètes : ils ne veulent rien lire et ils restent uniquement dans le cadre du dessin – c'est vrai que, la plupart du temps, ce n'est pas la peine de lire – mais de temps en temps, c'est important. Je dis souvent que la plupart des concours sont absolument comme si on faisait juger des opéras uniquement sur partition, par des gens qui ne savent pas lire le solfège, et, même s'ils savent le lire, qui n'entendent pas simultanément la musique et ne peuvent l'imaginer. Il y a une sorte de distorsion : si on prend un phénomène aussi simple que l'échelle, si on ne sait pas se remettre à l'échelle par rapport à un dessin, si on ne sait pas ce que quinze ou vingt-cinq mètres de haut veulent dire, alors on ne comprend plus rien, on n'est pas en mesure de se mettre en situation. Je crois que l'écrit est important pour compléter ces choses-là : il faut expliquer les choses la plupart du temps. Maintenant cette explication n'a un intérêt qu'à partir du moment où l'on a quelque chose à prouver – et je dirais que le drame de l'architecte, c'est qu'il faut toujours qu'il prouve. Il y a une sorte de méfiance institutionnalisée. Tout le monde semble vouloir comprendre, mais si seulement c'était vrai, si seulement tout le monde voulait comprendre et s'en donnait vraiment les moyens, en étant conscient de l'importance de l'enjeu. En fait dans les concours, l'explication des maîtres d'ouvrage n'est souvent qu'une première impression sur quelque chose qui est souvent trop complexe pour être compris en quelques secondes ou en quelques minutes. Et, effectivement, il n'y a que l'écrit qui, à un moment donné, peut rétablir un certain nombre d'intentions dans un degré de conscience vis-à-vis d'un projet qui n'est pas encore construit.

Le problème qu'on retrouve avec l'écrit, c'est que ce n'est pas une preuve et que les architectes nous ont habitués à des grandes déclarations, la plupart du temps lyriques et sans précision. Je veux dire que l'architecte est toujours suspecté de mentir. Et là aussi on devrait établir une certaine objectivité dans la lecture des textes. Il ne suffit pas de dire quelque chose, il faut voir si cela correspond à ce qui est là ; il ne faut pas se laisser abuser par l'auto-enthousiasme – peut-être légitime – de chaque architecte. Il y a une objectivité de l'écrit, comme il y a une objectivité du dessin ; il y a des choses qui sont là et des choses qui n'y sont pas. On ne peut pas dire n'importe quoi. En fin de compte il devrait y avoir des sanctions vis-à-vis de ceux qui disent n'importe quoi. La plupart des concours en France ne sont pas des concours avec des jurys culturels. Ce sont des gens qui soit savent trop bien ce qu'ils veulent, soit qui ne comprennent absolument pas ce qu'on leur dit, soit qui ont très peur de tout ce qu'on leur dit. Donc pour gagner un concours, il faut déjà qu'il y ait ce préalable, il faut qu'il s'agisse d'un concours d'architecture, où l'on parle d'architecture. Les seuls concours que j'ai pu gagner, sont des concours où l'enjeu était effectivement culturel, où j'avais en face de moi un jury qui se posait des questions de nature culturelle. Pour la présentation du projet de la Tour Sans Fins par exemple, il y avait une telle tension sur le projet et nous avions tellement travaillé dessus, que tout cela était naturel, mais j'ai eu la surprise de relire la transcription qu'en a fait François Chaslin et ce qui m'a surpris, c'est que cela ait l'air d'un texte construit, écrit, alors qu'il ne l'était pas. C'est sûr aussi que le non-dit fait partie de l'organisation du texte et de ce qui est suggéré. Mais cela, c'est vrai dans le dessin, c'est vrai dans le texte, c'est vrai dans la pensée et c'est vrai dans l'architecture par voie de conséquence. Tout n'est pas à dire, il y a des choses qui vont de soi, ou d'autres qui sont des conséquences au deuxième ou troisième degré.

Je crois que ce qui se passe aussi, c'est que l'on se construit soi-même : trois ou quatre cents projets, cela laisse évidemment des traces. Donc il y a une façon d'appréhender les choses, il y a une façon de réfléchir, une façon de prendre des raccourcis, il y a des convictions qui se créent. Ce qui veut dire que, quand Michel-Ange attaque un bloc de marbre à la fin de sa vie, on est à peu près sûr qu'il va en sortir quelque chose d'exceptionnel. Mais ce n'est pas dû au bloc de marbre, c'est dû au fait qu'il s'est sculpté lui-même – en plus du fait qu'il sait sculpter. C'est la même chose pour un architecte. C'est dans ce sens-là que l'on peut interpréter cette vieille histoire : un artiste passe sa vie à faire le même tableau. C'est d'ailleurs plus vrai pour un artiste que pour un architecte, parce qu'un artiste vit dans ses obsessions, alors qu'un architecte est toujours sollicité par l'extérieur. Mais quand même, il y a sûrement des attitudes communes qui font qu'on peut toujours dire que d'une certaine façon, il s'agit toujours d'une catégorie de projet, ou que c'est un projet vu sous cent incidences différentes. On ne peut pas sortir totalement de soi-même tout le temps, on est un peu prisonnier de ce qu'on s'est fait, de la façon dont on s'est fait, ou architecturé comme architecte.

C'est là une raison d'avoir un *sparring-partner* : il aide quelquefois à aller un peu plus loin, à changer de chemin. Et c'est un vrai débat. Quand je dis être pour la spécificité ou l'hyper-spécificité, ce n'est pas une lubie, c'est la conséquence d'un mode de pensée. Quand je vois la plupart des bâtiments basés sur des modèles culturels qui n'ont rien à voir avec l'endroit où ils ont été construits, je me demande ce que cela veut dire. Il y a eu là un vrai changement : je pense que si j'avais été architecte au XVIIIe siècle, j'aurais raisonné dans le sens d'une discipline autonome à travers des modèles culturels totalement admis, à travers des typologies qui faisaient tout à fait sens. On n'avait aucune raison de sortir de cela. Maintenant, avec l'éclatement urbain, chaque situation nécessite un diagnostic ; s'il n'y a pas ce diagnostic, on ne fait que des choses absurdes. On peut naturellement aller dans le sens de renforcer cette absurdité, on peut être un peu cynique, on peut trouver une beauté, à la limite, dans le côté le plus abrupt et le plus impensé, le plus automatique. Mais il doit me rester quelque chose des siècles précédents, parce que, bien que je ne pense pas en continuités et que je ne pense pas du tout que les modes urbains soient les mêmes, je pense toujours que, par rapport à une situation préexistante, on peut encore développer quelque chose qui soit de l'ordre du dialogue, du génie du lieu, qui soit de l'ordre de l'accent, qui soit de l'ordre d'un peu plus de poésie. Et si on sait faire cela, c'est déjà une raison de vivre. Sinon je crois que je ferais autre chose. J'ai deux philosophies : la première, c'est que cela ne sert à rien de faire une chose en laquelle on ne croit pas, uniquement pour construire. Il y a beaucoup d'architectes qui n'ont pas cette philosophie-là, qui pensent que c'est très important de construire – c'est très pragmatique car, aussi, il faut vivre. Mais si « il faut vivre » et si c'est la seule raison, alors il faut vivre d'autre chose. La deuxième chose, c'est qu'il faut que je prenne toutes les dispositions pour atteindre cette limite entre le possible et l'impossible. C'est comme si j'allais au bord d'un précipice et je voie le précipice arriver ; je cours et je vais de plus en plus lentement, jusqu'au moment où je vais mettre un pied dans le vide et... il ne faut pas que je mette les deux. Souvent je mets les deux. Je pense que, quand une chose est historiquement juste, c'est qu'elle est sur cette ligne-là, sur cette ligne qui fait qu'elle devient possible tout en étant improbable. On rend possible une chose qui est très incertaine. Et c'est là où l'acte architectural est exaltant.

J'ai cru un moment que cela allait être une attitude beaucoup plus dans l'esprit du temps et que j'avais peut-être seulement un petit décalage ; en fait je crains d'avoir un grand décalage. Je ne sais pas si c'est bon signe, parce que je ne sais pas si c'est être en avance ou simplement ne pas avoir l'heure. Quand on n'est pas à l'heure, on loupe tout simplement beaucoup de choses. Et ce métier est un métier où il faut faire passer les idées dans le réel : un architecte c'est un passeur, c'est quelqu'un qui a un passeport pour passer du virtuel au réel, pour faire passer du rêve à la réalité. C'est ce passage-là qui est intéressant. Donc, quand le décalage est trop grand avec ceux qui vous écoutent, et qui vous jugent, neuf fois sur dix cela ne passe pas. Et ce n'est pas que la langue soit une vraie barrière. Je vois avec mes amis japonais, on passe toujours par la traduction, mais je crois que ce qui est important à ce moment-là, c'est le désir et le plaisir de parler ensemble, cela ne nous empêche pas de rire, mais ce n'est pas la même vitesse, ce n'est pas une connivence immédiate. Donc il faut encore plus de volonté, ou plus de désir, pour se comprendre. Mais à partir du moment où ma philosophie est celle des particularismes et de la spécificité, moi cela me va très bien. Je n'attends pas des conditions suisses qu'elles soient des conditions françaises, cela me décevrait beaucoup. J'aime les différences, je n'ai vraiment aucun problème avec cela. Je dirais même que plus on me pousse à faire une chose d'une façon qui n'est pas automatiquement la mienne, plus cela m'intéresse. Effectivement, suivant les différents pays, ce ne sont pas les mêmes façons de réagir. Quelques fois il y a des difficultés, des choses qu'on ne comprend pas assez bien, quelques fois on va peut-être un peu moins loin. De toute façon, je suis vraiment persuadé qu'il n'y a pas d'architecture forte possible sans la rencontre d'un client et d'un architecte. C'est-à-dire qu'un architecte seul cela ne suffit pas, cela n'a jamais suffi.... Un client tout seul non plus d'ailleurs. Et il ne s'agit pas d'une question d'argent, mais plutôt d'une question d'adéquation. Si la personne pour qui vous travaillez ne comprend rien à ce que vous faites ou conteste tout ce que vous faites, tout se trouve limité, tout se trouve cassé, tout se trouve déformé. C'est pour cela qu'à chaque fois qu'un bâtiment est réussi, je suis très reconnaissant envers celui qui l'a fait avec moi, et je ne parle pas de mon équipe, je parle des clients : à Lucerne, sans Thomas Held, il n'y aurait pas de Centre de la Culture et des Congrès. C'est lui qui a cristallisé cela chez le client et qui a tout rendu possible. Il fallait une envie très forte, une compréhension, il fallait un feeling commun, il fallait une confiance, il fallait tout cela. Dans un projet comme celui-là, les rapports humains sont très importants. Quand je fais le parallèle avec le cinéma, il s'agit de cela aussi : on devrait avoir le générique d'un bâtiment. Brigitte Métra, qui est mon assistante à Lucerne, a tenu ce projet pendant longtemps et il y avait beaucoup de personnes avec elle, il y avait aussi les entreprises qui se sont passionnées. Donc un projet de cette ampleur, c'est une succession de volontés – de passions – focalisées sur un objectif. Et il appartient à un architecte de rendre cela possible, mais ce n'est pas toujours évident...

Sergio Cavero   *Que ressentez-vous à l'idée de photographier le Centre de la Culture et des Congrès, de fixer le bâtiment sur la pellicule ?*

Jean Nouvel   C'est finalement une chose assez naturelle, c'est d'ailleurs pour cela que je l'ai proposée. Je pense qu'il y a un certain nombre d'intentions conceptuelles qui peuvent être vérifiées postérieurement, ou prouvées par des photos. Mais il peut y avoir aussi des photos d'une nature assez conceptuelle, qui marquent les principales choses et qui vont sûrement dans le sens de cette approche un peu fractale. Ce n'est pas automatiquement la vue immédiate, c'est plutôt la mise en relation de plusieurs échelles, la mise en relation d'un site et d'un bâtiment. Donc, finalement, c'est une façon de lister, de relister les intentions du projet et de les donner à voir...

Version revue et corrigée d'un entretien avec Jean Nouvel le 9 juin 1998 à Paris, 10 cité d'Angoulême. Interlocuteur et rédacteur: Sergio Cavero (né à Neuchâtel, le 22. 9. 1969, architecte, depuis 1994 maître-assistant des Écoles Polytechniques Fédérales de Zurich [ETHZ] et de Lausanne [EPFL], il vit et travaille à Zurich).

Irene und Erich Lejeune, München
Christiane Leister, Stalden OW

Ruth Lay-Brun, Luzern
John Lay AG, Littau
Lawil AG, Littau
Dr. Kaspar Lang, Luzern
Beatrix und Dr. Victor Langenegger
Annemarie und Franz Kurzmeyer, Luzern
Kursaal-Casino AG, Luzern
Gerhard Kubers
Kuoni Reisen AG
Irene Kunde-Ernst Meyer

Stiftung Ch

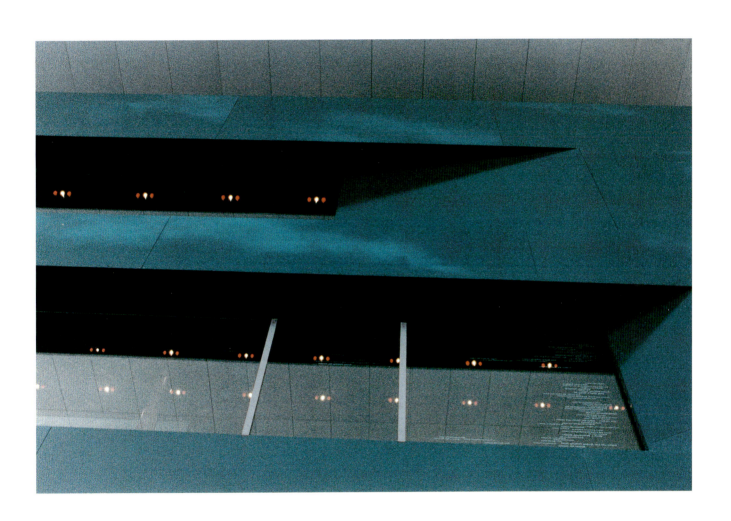

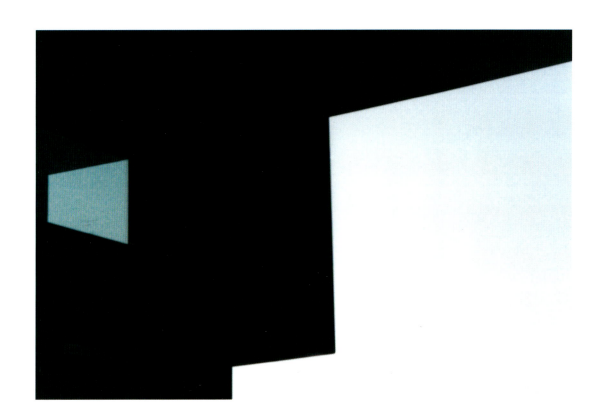

The Exact Representation of a Will

Sergio Cavero *Heinrich von Kleist writes in "Of the Progressive Constitution of Thoughts in Discourse"; "If you want to know something and you do not find it by meditation, I advise you, my friend, to talk about it with the next person that you meet"[1]. Do you recognise yourself in that reflection? Which use do you make of discussion and of speech in your design process? Which are the salient phases of it and what are the consequences of this way of proceeding?*

Jean Nouvel Each time that we begin a project, it is about flushing out all the good reasons to do it. In this sense the analysis is the basis of the project. I am indeed on the opposite of any architectural creation based upon an immediate creative intuition, upon an innate talent which would allow to find alone, in oneself, the reasons and the values of a project. Talent – which is a suspicious word in my eyes – all the same it is always much will, and the project, is often the exact representation of a will. If there is no will, there is no project. I believe therefore that it is very important to give oneself, above all, the means to see and to know. Seeing because we actually capture objective and subjective things, and knowing, because there are other things that we cannot know if we don't go looking for them, whether being of the order of history, whether being of economic or human order. All these things are not seen immediately. Thus, when I begin an important project, I try to gather a maximum of information. That reminds me of what Buckminster Fuller used to say: «I am not very intelligent, but I am well-informed.» As soon as we are well-informed, it is already somewhat better. That does not mean that we are going to get there, but means that we have more chance of getting there. On important projects, such as competitions with complex programmes, I form a team of analysts, except of course if

---

1. «Wenn du etwas wissen willst und es durch Meditation nicht finden kannst, so rate ich dir, mein lieber, sinnreicher Freund, mit dem nächsten Bekannten, der dich aufstösst, darüber zu sprechen. [...]», Heinrich von Kleist *in* Über die allmähliche Verfertigung der Gedanken beim Reden, 1805/06, (vol. 7, 2nd Edition, Kleist «Werke und Briefe», publ. by Erich Schmidt and Georg Minde-Pouet).

it is a very small and simple project of which I see the ins and outs and for which I am not going to put together a group of ten people.

The other aspect of the question is that, when the information arrives, of course, it is discussed by the team, we have brainstorming sessions, but, whatever the diagnosis that we are led to make, it has to be tested. That is why I have always needed what I call a «sparring partner», who is someone that I choose upon very particular criteria: it has to be someone who has a different culture from my own. In a certain way, I am a vampire; I vampirise his culture. People who have fulfilled this very role, are very specific people: Jacques Le Marquet – who was the scenographer of Jean Vilar – who is a writer for the theatre and who thus has a theatrical, scenographic, literary, visual culture, that I absolutely do not have; it was Olivier Boissière who is firstly an art critic – of plastic arts and architecture – who is also a writer and who has a literary culture that I do not have, that I did not have, and that I will certainly never have. Olivier Boissière worked with me during seven or eight years. Now, it is Hubert Tonka, who is a philosopher, who is an editor and who has a complementary outlook to mine and a different culture, that I do not have automatically.

Thus, there is a confrontation of two cultural points of view: when I emit a hypothesis, I like to confront it to this first judgement, to this first filter, and often this sends me back to something of which I had not thought. Then all this happens also on the register, it too a strong carrier of dynamics, of friendship. I believe that we only make worthwhile things when it gives pleasure and that if one is really bored, it shows in what one is going to produce. If there is an optimistic dimension in all this – a warmth – it is found back in all that we do. There needs to be enthusiasm, and I cultivate this enthusiasm, this pleasure of living: often, these brainstorming sessions or meetings with my sparring partner, take place around a table, with a good bottle between us, in restaurants or late at night.

There is an implication in the project, which means that, when a project develops, we live good spells, that is to say we often see each other, or we call each other on the phone, because we had an idea about something, or we just meet each other at the office with the team. Pressure builds up, there is a kind of optimism and all the hypotheses burst forth around the table, the only problem being to catch them in their flight. It is finally about a whole series of actions, incidents, of reactions, and I believe that it is very important to talk, to put forward a certain number of hypotheses, of opinions, or of judgements. In the end, the important thing is not so much what we put on the table at first: what counts, is to put something there and then after to shape it. Even if we say something stupid, something interesting can come out of it after five or six reflections, after five or six criticisms. This is my own method and I am not sure that it is totally original, but in most cases, it corresponds to my character, it corresponds to my philosophy of work and it opens up onto often unpredictable things.

Finally, this is what is interesting; it is the adventure of each instant in life. If there is not this adventure, if I do not know that at each moment I can change my opinion, if I do not know that at each moment one can bring me a piece of information helping me to evolve, I am going to reproduce what I already know – and in the end, it will be an exercise of pure narcissism or the expression of a fixed personality, who perhaps evolves, but in autarky. I am therefore against autarky, I am for this opening and from there a certain number of methods arise. We try for example to make lists: everything that should not be done, because it is foolish; everything that we would like to do, even if it is impossible. On one side, there are wishes, there are absolute desires, and on the other the things one should not get into. It is a bit caricatured, but it helps to sort things out, and sometimes we put everything back in question, we say «why¿»: it is this very process that leads to the project.

We can never do without the most objective analysis, without a kind of sieve; first one needs to see everything and then one needs to evoke in a generic way a certain number of hypotheses. Once we have done that, obviously we look for things that are tangible. Firstly we look for the synthesis of all that, which is a problem much harder to solve, as in chess. Once we have done that, we realise that we have a base, but in fact, the essential is not yet there. Thus it can happen afterwards: after we evoke these kinds of things, and the work on a project is a lengthy process, there are many stages, there are things that are superimposed, that contradict themselves at a certain point, it is not at all linear. Thus in the end, we talk about everything! This reminds me of what happened in regards to a housing project: I wanted to get out of the housing standard in France and I was talking about it with Jacques Le Marquet and we were virtually doing a narrative architecture. Because everything was based on the functionalist approach, we began to imagine the worst scenarios: a murder in the apartment, the way one would get out of there if one committed a burglary. A whole series of things that had nothing to do with functionality, but was a manner in which to put back a little humanity in the project, because the objective matter was uninispiring.

The architect is in a very special position, he is the one who organises the method that will allow him to go the furthest, to advance the farthest possible in the project. But in contrast to this there is a lot of agitation, all these discussions. One must put them both side by side: there must be silence, there must be concentration, one must think over all the arguments. Once all the analyses are there, and all the reasoning has taken place, one must choose. It is what I call a creative leap. Then, even if I fight against intuition, as long as possible, this doesn't mean to say that I object to it, as I know well that at one point, I will propose something that will not be entirely of the order of analysis, that will not be entirely the product of a deduction. There is thus a moment where, in opposite to this agitation, I find myself generally in bed and I begin; I need twenty, twenty-five minutes of good concentration and from there, during one or two hours, the clockwork runs smoothly: there are accelerations, there are exaltations, I think that I have found it, I am not sure, and finally I say: that is it. I need to know that the chronometer is ticking, to know that the next day will be the last moment to make a choice. There is in this something quite risky, but for me, it is a limited risk, in the sense that I have held to the most solid things as long as possible. I am in a certain way already channelled: I have already gone the furthest I could in the things that make the most sense.

This creative leap touches most often the problem of formalisation. One thing which is very difficult, I think, – and it is because of this that perhaps all the architects do not play this game – is that one has to counter the permanent desire to quickly formalise. It is to say that if one is a formalist architect, one knows already which form one will make, because there is only this form which satisfies us, which interests us; in the same way as an artist in the domain of the plastic arts, we want to do our thing all white, a thing all round, a thing all triangular, a thing all square. We want to do it, thus we know we are going to get there. I try not to do this, and I would even say that I manage to find pleasure, perhaps a bit masochist, to delay this choice as much as possible: I do not want to know the form, as long as I do not know all the rest. This creative leap is in fact the first formal choice: considering what I know of the programme, of the site, of the cultural habits, of the budget, of all the parameters at stake, I am going to choose a formalisation. But even when I start from the form, in the spirit of a formalisation, it is not however defined. We have made a step and we move towards something that will be refined, will be sharpened, and gradually the form is going to be enriched. I am anyway not someone who goes from the global to the particular. When one takes the spirit of something, one often sees that one can begin with the spirit of an interior or by focusing on something, for example.

A point which constantly questions me and which is strategically very important, is the fact of seizing the qualities of a situation. If I have placed the Institute of the Arab World close to the Seine, when I was asked to put it on the other side, and if I wanted it higher than the building regulations permit, it is so that the building manages to obtain a view it otherwise would never have had. If I place myself in Lucerne on a corner and if I open that corner, it is to have a panoramic view both of the city and of the lake which gives something which does not exist and which is difficult to obtain. One cannot say that this is literal architecture, because it is not the form itself which is there, it is simply that the building obtains this additional quality. If I place myself facing Lucerne and if I cut up postcards, it is because I know that I have that and that I know which scale I have before me and thus I place myself in a position to obtain and to take on meaning in relation to a general site or a landscape. It is all these elements, which thus become strategic choices and which only then lead to forms. It is for this reason that I cannot have a single column in Lucerne: if I have a column marring this panoramic view, I look like a fool...What is beautiful, is this pan from the mountain to the old bridge: there is no other place in Lucerne which possesses this. Thus, if I offer this, I already offer an exceptional architecture in its strategy. All the choices, made after the development of the project, are strategic choices, but they are also formal choices, which can start from an interior, which can start from a spirit of detail related to a place which will have struck me in the city and that I am going to extrapolate, but which can also start, on the contrary, from a general volumetry that I will find, in relationship with the rest.

I believe a great deal in the fractal approach, that is to say that there is nothing more inept in architecture – particularly these last years – than the notion of enlarged models. Although certain people do that very well, a simple enlarged model is something appalling, because it does not evoke any emotion related to distance, related to touch or related to detail. What I like, are the ruptures of scale in the fractal approach, that make us move from one world to another, from an aesthetic emotion, or from a register to another. While keeping the spirit of the project, which is precisely going to be this relationship between these different layers, I will discover things which have nothing to do with one another. For example, if I look at you from above, I see a beautiful black head, if I get close, I am going to begin to see glasses from above, then if I get closer, I am going to see hair planted in pores, then if I get inside, it will be cells: it is always going to be something else. But the views are not taken into account: it is not about the same image which is enlarged, because I am going to discover each time a formal and emotional register which will be of a very different nature. If we go back to the example of Lucerne, the fact of having a birds-eye view from above, is one thing, but the fact of reading from the bridge a line and an angle, is something else, and if, under the overhang, I see all the glazed panels accumulate on each side, it is again another thing: each time, I go from one world to another in relation to this displacement and to this proximity of the view. What I elaborate once all the elements of the analysis are there, through a strategy, is first a few formal aspects and it is in these formal aspects or in this formal strategy, that I later develop projects within the project, or sensations within sensations, in relation to a distant, close, interior, exterior view, etc. All these view-angles in the project are things that characterise what I call a conceptual architecture. It can be called something else, but it means that there is only the spirit and only a totally thought out strategy that can allow one to get to that in a convincing way.

In fact, I am glad if a project can be ten thousand projects simultaneously. There is no relationship between the unity of the project and the fact that it has this complexity. The modern era wanted an object to be readable, decipherable, everything to be based on purity, that there would not be anything afterwards. Today, we can play on a conceptual unity, on an idea which runs through the whole project, but as soon as we move through the project, we discover many things that reinforce each other. It is the pleasure of discovery, it is the pleasure to glance over an unexpected thing, but I am not talking here about something which would be automatically based on affirmed discontinuity or on heterogeneity. I speak of something which has enough depth to be seen in many different ways. Finally – and it is also here an old debate – I consider that a work of art is precisely what stands up to contemplation, that means that if there is no mystery, we can say that a work of art is dead. A work of art must be able to touch all sorts of people – whatever their orientation or cultural level: the great masterpieces of literature or painting are accessible to all, though perhaps not in the same way: in «La Chartreuse de Parme» you can see a simple love story, a whole approach on Italy, a whole metaphysics, it can be read at different levels. When we see great works of painting, it is a similar thing: the slightest detail, a hand for example, in the way it is painted, in its expression, without having seen the whole work, you already know that it is a good work and you know that you are going to see many other things. In architecture, it is quite similar. It is fundamentally about a problem of resistance: I remember this discussion I had with Jacques Le Marquet, who always used to tell me: «How deep does a treasure need to be buried in order for it to be discovered?». Yes, it has to be discovered, but not totally...

I often say that an architect, is an amplifier, he is someone who is going to capture emotions or sensations and who is asking himself: «what can I do with that?» If in the end this emotion has been strong enough for me, I am going to crystallise myself on it and I am going to amplify it, so that nobody can miss it: if I am interested in it, I am going to oblige everybody to look. Accordingly, if everybody looks, everybody must find this beautiful, because this has touched me, because I have been moved, but there will be a lot of people who will find it absolutely uninteresting. I therefore have no vocation towards cultural consensus; we cannot have the pretention to please everybody. An architectural work, like a work of art, is a commitment, but the various messages or the various sensations we programme have to touch their goal. Foremost, they must be readable – and when I say readable, it does not mean written on it in large letters – it means that they are being captured. From there on the building lives its life: from the moment we have found a certain number of sensory elements that are somewhat new, we are almost sure to shock a certain number of people, because there is a convention of sensation, a convention of art and if we are beside it, we can almost be certain that there will be a resistance. Contrary to what people think, we do not look for this resistance, we do not attempt to shock the bourgeois. Simply, if these things correspond to a truth of the author and if they moreover correspond to a reality related to an era, or to things that everybody perceives, there might be a chance that what touches us, also touches the others. Thus, these choices are made on the basis of these very reasons and not at all in order to go towards this cultural consensus which is a kind of soft consensus. We very well know that every creation – in the real sense of the term – is at first an aggression and that, only gradually, perhaps not in one go, the visitor has to be familiarised; in this way the starting point becomes progressively something which is more acceptable. The convention of beauty is a terrible question: when Wim Wenders – whom I appreciate, began to look at macadam, electric lines and things like that, it was poetry which was, most of the time, inaccessible to the passer-by: it had to be distanced in order that we finally realised what it concealed. These poetics of everyday life, while things are under our eyes, could not imprint us, could not reach us, all this was transparent for us: this distance which allows us to look at the thing in another way and to capture its beauty, has to always be created. I think anyway that if we want to create the most permanent building – and it is the only permanence there is in architecture –, it has to be adequate, and above all to be loved. We always believe that the way to do the most perennial building is to make it in granite or concrete; on the contrary, we have to see to it that, very quickly, it becomes the symbol of an attitude towards an epoch: from this moment on everybody cherishes it. That is why often the most difficult years for a building are the first twenty or thirty years, because, it is not yet respected. But, as soon as we begin to understand what it means in relation to something fairly rare, fairly precise – fairly precious –, at this moment, as fragile as it may be, it has taken off for a certain time.

It has often been said that I work with words, which is true. But words, what does it mean? It simply means thought. If we speak, we speak a language, and language is made to communicate and to exchange: to accelerate and to clarify a formalisation process. I have always loathed people who decide before knowing what they have to do. This was my first problem at the Beaux Arts School, I fought against what I called the «sketching intuition»: one follows his pencil all the time, one makes a little doodle, then one makes another one and another one and another one, and then finally, one will feel the automatic indulgence that we have with ourselves, that means that as soon as we make three nice lines together, we are going to say: «ah, so that's it, it was very simple and it is very beautiful»… I am strongly suspicious of anything that is hurried formalisation and formalisation which is not sustained by a true will. Thus, it is in this sense that I object to a form of intuition, whether this intuition be in the head or, which is even more dangerous, as soon as it is translated by a formalisation, which finally is similar to reading teacups. I have seen so many projects at the Beaux Arts School that were graphic splendours, but where there was absolutely nothing likely to give them this very strength, once they would have passed into reality. There is a huge difference between a graphic culture and an architectural culture, between writing a score and the music that we are going to hear, once it will be interpreted. At this point, what we call words are important: thanks to them, I try not to be abused, words are there to detect the traps. This without being absolutist: when we need a sketch to be understood, so, we make a sketch. As soon as we get into the formalisation phase, all the things have to be in place and the drawing must not act as a constraint, it must not be a problem, it has to be uninhibited: it will be a simple means, that we master completely. But I know that every time I search for something by drawing, it is that I am not through with my project. I often say to the architects here that when we look for a facade, it is because something is not right. We never have to look for a facade. Either the thing is there, or it is not: as soon as we search for a facade, it is because we have nothing to say, it means that the programme is not there – I am talking about the programme of what we are drawing – and it means that it is not flowing. We often scare ourselves with drawing. I remember the first time I saw the plans of the Cartier Foundation, or even the drawing of the south facade of the Institute of the Arab World, with this very dense grid: people that were going by me used to say: «Poor man, this is really not possible...». It is hopeless to have to explain one's thinking in such a way to an architect from the French Building Department: there is always an uneasiness. Obviously, what is important is not the grid, but it is what we are going to see inside, it is what we are going to see through, it is what is programmed or not. Often the drawing does not say a quarter of what it contains. It is a tool to represent and produce, but it has to represent an idea. Often it has to be completed by texts. Anyway there are things which lend themselves more to drawing than others: the more primary the thing is, the more it can be symbolised by a drawing. We can say this for a certain opaque classical architecture, based on volumes, on shadow, and light in the sense of mass, projected shadow, own shadow, etc. But as soon as we get into notions of depth, of reflection, of variations of architecture with light, with time, with seasons, this is not sufficient anymore. One must set into motion a whole system which is so economically heavy, it is no longer absolutely manageable. Thus we function differently.

I am suspicious of everything that fixes. But I also reflect by writing – I can deepen a thought through writing – and I consider that on projects, texts are often as important or more important than drawings, or at least strictly complementary. What upsets me, after having spent a good portion of my architectural experience on juries, is that I realise that writings have absolutely no weight. When I am on an architectural jury – I often fight because of that –, it seems that we are dealing with illiterates: they do not want to read anything and they only remain within the frame of the drawing – it is true that, most of the time, it is not worth reading – but from time to time, it is important. I often say that most competitions are as if operas were only judged on the score, by people that cannot read notation, and, even if they know how to read it, they do not hear the music simultaneously and they cannot imagine it. There is a kind of distortion: if we take a phenomenon as simple as scale, if we do not know how to put ourselves back to scale in relation to a drawing, if we do not know what fifteen or twenty-five meters high means, then we do not understand anything anymore, we are unable to position ourselves. I think that writing is important to complement these things: we need to explain things most of the time. This explanation only has an interest from the moment that we have something to prove – and I would say that the drama of the architect, is that he always has to prove. There is a kind of institutionalised mistrust. Everybody seems to want to understand, but if only it were true, if only everybody wanted to understand and really apply themselves, being aware of the importance of the stakes. In fact in competitions, the explanation of the client is often just a first impression on something which is often too complex to be understood in a few seconds or in a few minutes. Actually, there is only writing which, at a given moment, can re-establish a certain number of intentions in a degree of consciousness towards a project which is not yet built.

The problem encountered in writing, is that it is not a proof and that architects have accustomed us to great declarations, most of the time lyrical and precisionless. I mean to say that the architect is always suspected of lying. There too, we should establish a certain objectivity in the reading of texts. It is not enough to say something, we have to see if it corresponds to what is there; we must not let ourselves be abused by the auto-enthusiasm – perhaps legitimate – of each architect. There is an objectivity of writing, as there is an objectivity of drawing: there are things that are there and things that are not. We cannot say anything. In the end there should be sanctions against the ones that say anything. Most competitions in France are not competitions with cultural juries. They are people who know too well what they want, who either do not understand absolutely what we tell them, or who are very worried about everything we tell them. So in order to win a competition, there already needs to be this prerequisite, it has to be an architectural competition where we talk about architecture. The only competitions I have won, are competitions where the stakes were really cultural, where I had in front of me a jury which was asking questions of a cultural nature. For the presentation of the Tour

Sans Fins[2] project, for example, there was such tension around the project, and we had worked so hard, that all of this was normal, but I was surprised to reread the transcription that François Chaslin made of it and what surprised me, was that it looked like a constructed text, written, even though it was not. Also, it is for sure that what is left unsaid belongs to the organisation of the text and to what is suggested. But this is true in drawing, it is true in text, it is true in thought and it is true in architecture by consequence. There are things which are better left unsaid, there are things which are obvious, or others that are second or third degree consequences.

I think that what also happens, is that one builds oneself: three or four hundred projects, obviously leave traces. Thus there is a way to apprehend things, a way to think, a way to take shortcuts, there are convictions which are being created. Which means that, when Michelangelo confronts a block of marble at the end of his life, we are almost certain that something exceptional is going to come out of it. But this is not due to the block of marble, it is due to the fact that he has sculpted himself – on top of the fact that he knows how to sculpt. It is the same thing for an architect. It is in this sense that we can interpret this old story: an artist spends his life painting the same picture. Anyway, it is more true for an artist than for an architect, because an artist lives in his obsessions, while an architect is always solicited by the exterior. But anyhow, there are certainly shared attitudes which allow us to say in a certain way, that it is always about a category of project, or that it is a project seen under a hundred different incidences. We cannot totally get out of ourselves all the time, we are the prisoners of what we made of ourselves, of the way we made ourselves, or architectured as architects.

This is the reason to have a «sparring – partner»: he sometimes helps to go a little further, to change path. It is a real debate. When I say that I am for specificity or hyper-specificity, it is not a whim, it is the consequence of a mode of thinking. When I see most buildings based on cultural models that have nothing to do with the place where they have been built, I wonder what it means. There has been a real

2. Literally : Endless Tower

change: I think that had I been an architect in the eighteenth century, I would have reasoned in the sense of an autonomous discipline through fully admitted cultural models, through typologies that were making complete sense. There were no reasons to get out of that. Now, with the urban explosion, each situation necessitates a diagnosis; if there is not this diagnosis, we only do absurd things. We can naturally go in the direction of reinforcing this absurdity, we can be a bit cynical, we can find beauty, on the edge, in the most abrupt and the most unthought, the most automatic side. But something from the previous centuries must remain, because, even though I do not think in continuities and that I do not think at all that urban modes are the same, I always think that, in relation to a pre-existing situation, we can still develop something which is of the order of the dialogue, of genius of place, which is of the order of accent, which is of the order of a little more poetry. If we know how to do that, it is already a reason to live. Otherwise I think I would do something else. I have two philosophies: the first, is that there is no need to do something in which we do not believe, only in order to build. There are many architects that do not have this philosophy, who think that it is very important to build – it is very pragmatic because, also, one needs to make a living. But if «one needs to make a living» and if it is the only reason, then one needs to make a living from something else. The second thing, is that I need to take all the dispositions to reach the limit between the possible and the impossible. It is as if I were going to the edge of a precipice and that I see the precipice approach: I run and then I go slower and slower until the moment when I am going to put one foot into the void and ... I must not put both. Often I put both. I think that, when something is historically right, it is because it is on that very line, on the line which makes it become possible while being improbable. We make possible something which is very uncertain. This is where the architectural act is exalting.

    I believed for a while that this would be an attitude much more in the spirit of time and that I perhaps had only a small time-lag; in fact I worry about having a large time-lag. I do not know if it is a good sign, because I do not know if it is to be ahead or simply not to know what time it is. When we are not on time, we simply miss many things. This profession is one where one has to convey one's ideas: an architect is a conveyor, it is someone who has a passport to go from the virtual to the real, to pass from the dream to the reality. It is this passage which is interesting. Thus, when the gap is too large with those who listen to you, and those who judge, nine times out of ten it does not work. It is not that language is a real barrier. I see with my Japanese friends, we always go through translation, but I believe that what is important at this moment, is the desire and the pleasure to talk together, it does not prevent us from laughing, but it is not the same speed, it is not an immediate accord. Thus there needs to be even more will, or more desire, to understand each other. For the moment my philosophy is one of particularisms and of specificity, it suits me very well. I do not expect Swiss conditions to be French conditions, I would be very disappointed. I like differences, I really do not have any problems with that. I would even say that the more I am pushed to do something in a way which is not automatically mine, the more I become interested. Actually, depending on different countries, there are not the same ways to react. Sometimes there are difficulties, things that we do not understand well enough, perhaps sometimes we do not go so far. Anyhow, I am persuaded that there is no strong architecture possible without the meeting of a client and an architect. It is to say that an architect alone is not enough, it has never been enough… Neither a client alone. It is not about a question of money, but rather about a question of adequacy. If the person for whom you work does not understand what you are doing, everything is limited, everything is broken, everything is deformed. This is why each time a building is a success, I am very grateful towards the person who did it with me, and I am not talking about my team, I am talking about clients: in Lucerne, without Thomas Held, there would not be a Culture and Congress Center. He is the one who crystallised this with the client and who made everything possible. There had to be a very strong desire, a comprehension, there needed to be a common feeling, there needed to be confidence, there needed to be all of that. In a project like this one, the human relations are very important. When I make the parallel with cinema, it is also about that: we should have credits for a building. Brigitte Metra, who is my assistant in Lucerne, held that project for a long time and there were many people with her, there were also the the extremely enthusiastic builders. Thus a project of this scale, is a succession of wills – of passions – focalised upon an objective. Only an architect can make that possible but it is not always easy...

Sergio Cavero *How do you feel about the idea of photographing the Culture and Congress Center, of freezing the building on film.*

Jean Nouvel It is finally a fairly natural thing, this is anyway why I have suggested it. I think there are a certain number of conceptual intentions that can be verified subsequently, or proved by photos. But there can also be photos of a fairly conceptual nature, that indicate the principal things and surely go in the direction of this slightly fractal approach. It is not automatically the immediate view, it is rather to put into relation many scales, to put into relation a site and a building. Thus, finally, it is a way of making lists, and remaking lists of the intentions of a project and making them be seen...

Edited text from an interview with Jean Nouvel held at 10 cité d'Angoulême in Paris on June 9, 1998. Conduct of interview and text editing by Sergio Cavero (architect born in Neuchâtel 22. 9. 1969; assistant at the Swiss Institute of Technology in Zurich, ETHZ, and Lausanne, EPFL since 1994; lives and works in Zurich).

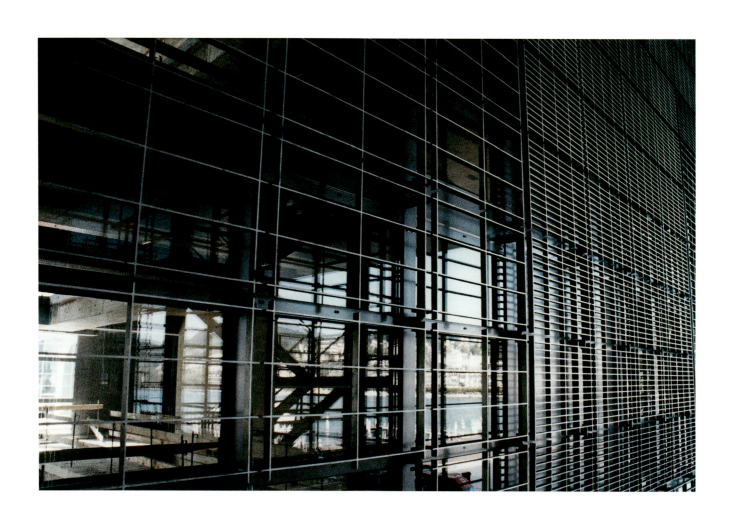

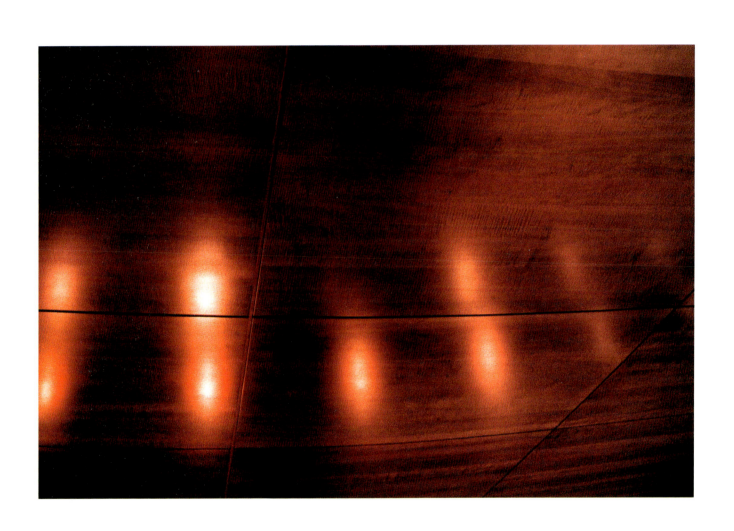

Projects in Switzerland by Jean Nouvel

1989
Ackermann Factory in Entlebuch

Cartier-Interdica Factory in Villarts-en-Glane

1990
Landis & Gyr Headquarters in Zug

Renovation and extension of the GWF Factory in Lucerne

1991
Cartier Factory in Villeret

1992
Urban project on an industrial site in Winterthur

1993
Extension of the Swiss Institute of Technology in Lausanne

1996
Airport in Zurich

1997
Stadium in Geneva

Credits «Culture and Congress Center»

Client
Trägerstiftung Kultur und Kongreßzentrum Luzern (Suisse)

Architect
Architectures Jean Nouvel

Project architect AJN
Brigitte Métra

Assistants to project architect
Joëlle Achache, Marie-Hélène Baldran, Didier Brault, Sandro Carbone, Günther Domenig, Xavier Lagurgue, Denis Laurent, Philippe Mathieu, Éric Nespoulous, Julie Parmentier, Matthias Raasch, Markus Rëthlisberger, Beth Weinstein, Stefan Zopp

General contractor and coordinator
ARGE, Electrowatt Engineering AG - Göhner Merkur AG

Engineers
Structural — Electrowatt Engineering AG et Plüss + Meyer Bauingenieure AG
General coordination and
Sanitary — Schudel & Schudel Ing. SIA
Mechanical — Aicher, De Martin, Zweng AG, Balduin-Weisser
Electrical — Scherler AG
Audiovisual — Infraplan
Scenography — Planungsgruppe AB

Consultants
Scenography — Jacques Le Marquet
Acoustical — Russell Johnson - ARTEC
Yann Kersalé
Hubert Tonka

Painting, colours, plastic interventions
Alain Bony, Henri Labiole

Signalisation
SRPC/Rüegg

Dates
Beginning of the studies: June 1992
Summary preliminary project: July 1993
Construction permit: November 1994
Beginning of the construction: January 1995
Tender documents completed: March 1995
Construction documents: 1996–97
Completion of the first construction phase: August 1998
Second construction phase: December 1999

Programme
Culture and Congress Centre comprises:
1 symphony hall (1900 seats)
1 rehearsal room
1 multi-purpose hall (900 seats)
1 congress hall (300 seats), 8 conference rooms and exhibition foyers
1 museum: 2400 sq. meters of exhibition space, 400 sq. meters of reception space
180 sq. meters of administration space, 630 sq. meters of related spaces
3 restaurant/catering spaces, dressing rooms, offices and service spaces

Usable floor area
22 000 sq. meters

Gross floor area
35 000 sq. meters

Budget
200 000 000 Sfr. (approximately 850 000 000 FF) (all expenses taken into account)

Perspectives
Vincent Lafont

Models
Etienne Follenfant

Photos
Philippe Ruault

106
*Plans
Sections
Elevations*

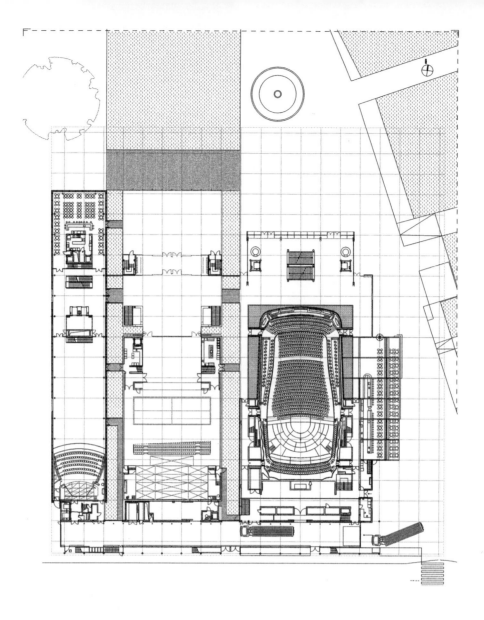

*ground
floor plan*
1/1000

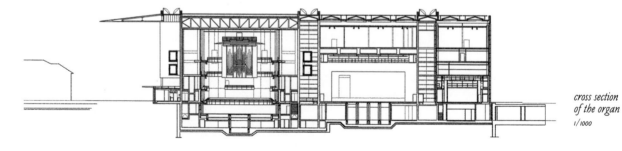

*cross section
of the organ*
1/1000

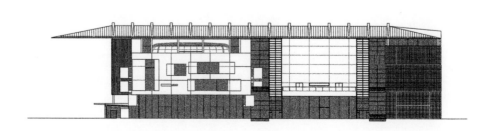

north elevation
1/1000

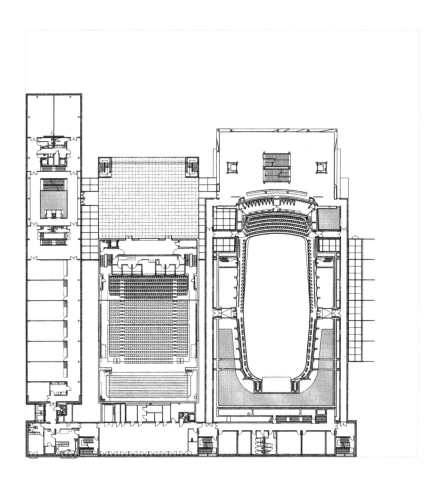

second floor plan
1/1000

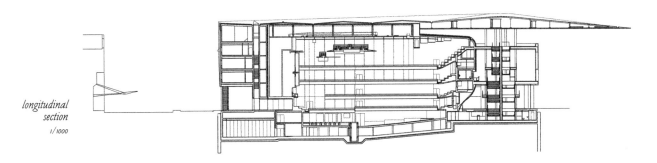

longitudinal section
1/1000

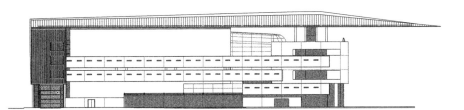

east elevation
1/1000

107
Plans
Sections
Elevations

108
Plans
Sections
Elevations

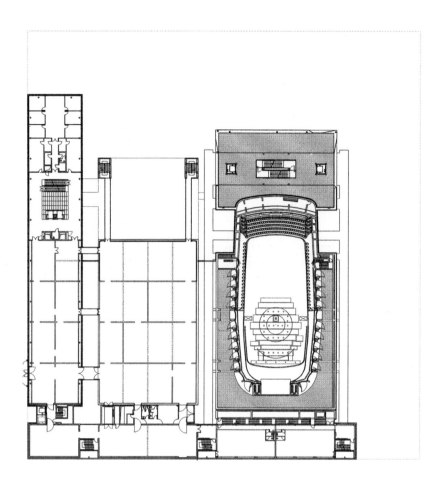

*fourth
floor plan*
1/1000

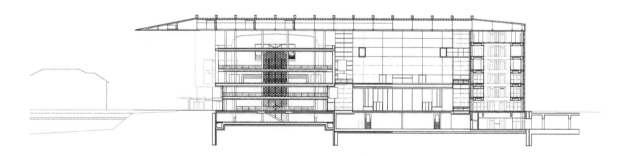

*cross section
of the foyers*
1/1000

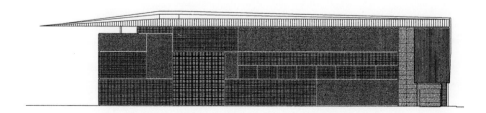

west elevation
1/1000

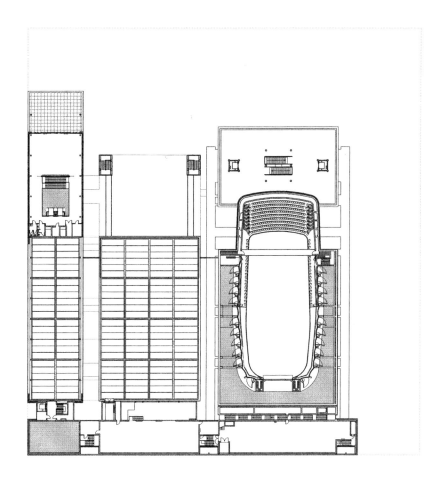

fifth floor plan
1/1000

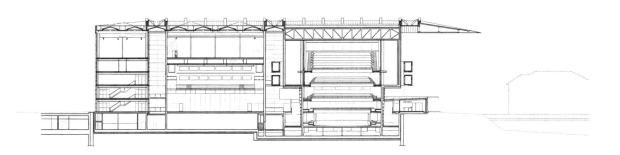

cross section of the hall
1/1000

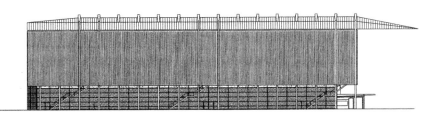

south elevation
1/1000

109
Plans
Sections
Elevations

Jean Nouvel
born in 1945 at Fumel

PRINCIPAL WORKS

1998

75 Housing Units
1000 square meters of commercial space; Vienna, Austria

1996

Friedrichstadt Passages
Galeries Lafayette department store integrated into a complex of boutiques, night club, housing, offices, and parking; Berlin, Germany

1995

Cartier Foundation
cultural space for contemporary art; boulevard Raspail; Paris

1994

Triangle des Gares
shopping centre; Lille

1993

Lyon Opera House
1300 person hall, 200 person amphitheatre; Lyon
This building received the Equerre d'Argent prize, 1993

Cartier CTL
watch factory; Saint Imier, Switzerland

International Congress Centre
3 halls: seating for 2000, 750, and 350 persons; Tours

Christopher Columbus Residence
107 social housing units, offices, retail; Bezons

1992

CLM BBDO
headquarters of an advertising agency; Issy-les-Moulineaux

Les Thermes
90 room, 3-star hotel; centre for balneotherapy; Dax

1991

Pierre et Vacances
174 housing units; Cap d'Ail

1989

Hôtel Saint-James
Saint-James Hotel
18 room, 4-star hotel, restaurant St-James. J.-M. Amat; Bouliac
Architectural Record prize

Onyx
cultural centre, 600 person hall; Saint Herblain

INIST
scientific and technical documentation centre for the CNRS; Nancy

1987

Nemausus
114 social housing units; Nîmes

Arab World Institute
quai d'Austerlitz; Paris
This building received the Equerre d'Argent prize, 1987

WORKS AND PROJECTS IN PROGRESS

1998

Mediapark Block 1
offices, apartment hotel, retail, schools (construction in progress); Cologne, Germany

Victoria Building
building including parking, retail, offices (construction in progress); Frankfurt, Germany

Cité Judiciaire
including: county court, magistrates court, court of assizes (construction in progress); Nantes

Cognacq-Jay Foundation
extension of a retirement home (completion 1998) and refurbishment (in progress); Rueil-Malmaison

Interunfall
headquarters of an insurance company (construction in progress); Bregenz, Austria

Andel Building
offices and retail; Prague, Czech Republic

Bateaux-Mouches Company
building, offices; Prague, Czech Republic

Gallo-Roman Museum
Périgueux

Gasometer
transformation of a gasometer into housing and shopping centre; Vienna, Austria

Museum of Advertising
Louvre Museum; Paris

Scientific Forum
scientific adventure park; Frameries, Belgium

Expo 2000
scenography of the exhibition "Mobility"; Hanover, Germany

Expo 2000
scenography of the exhibition "The future of Work"; Hanover, Germany

Shiodome Project
office tower; Tokyo, Japan

110 Buildings & projects

Dank

Wir danken Jean Nouvel, Brigitte Métra, Charlotte Kruk und Hubert Tonka für die intensive und freundschaftliche Zusammenarbeit bei der Realisierung von Ausstellung und Katalog, Inès Lamunière für die Einführung anläßlich der Vernissage vom 26. September 1998, Sergio Cavero für die sorgfältige Bearbeitung des Gespräches mit Jean Nouvel, Nani Moras für die präzise Abschrift des Textes ab Band, Lydia Roduit für die Nachkontrollen der Texte, Marco Battaglia, Monika Künzler-Deon, Walter Lenggenhager und Anna Marie Wirz-Kupper für besondere organisatorische und administrative Unterstützung, Robert Steiger und Karoline Mueller-Stahl für das verständnisvolle Lektorat, Stefan Zopp für die Unterstützung im Rahmen des AJN, Büro Luzern.

Architekturgalerie Luzern, 28. August 1998

Remerciements

Nous tenons à remercier Jean Nouvel, Brigitte Métra, Charlotte Kruk et Hubert Tonka pour leur active et amicale collaboration en vue de la réalisation de l'exposition et de son catalogue, Inès Lamunière pour sa présentation lors du vernissage du 26 septembre 1998, Sergio Cavero pour la préparation minutieuse de son entretien avec Jean Nouvel, Nani Moras pour la transcription du texte, Lydia Roduit pour sa vérification, Marco Battaglia, Monika Künzler-Deon, Walter Lenggenhager et Anna Marie Wirz-Kupper pour leur soutien dans l'administration et l'organisation, Robert Steiger et Karoline Mueller-Stahl pour leur lecture intelligente, Stefan Zopp pour son aide dans le cadre AJN/bureau de Lucerne.

Galerie d'Architecture Lucerne, 28 août 1998

Acknowledgements

We would like to express our thanks to Jean Nouvel, Brigitte Métra, Charlotte Kruk and Hubert Tonka for their intense and friendly collaboration for the realisation of the exhibition and catalogue, Inès Lamunière for the introduction on the occasion of the opening on September 26, 1998, Sergio Cavero for the careful editing of the interview with Jean Nouvel, Nani Moras for the precise transcription of the text from the taped version, Lydia Roduit for the rereading of the French text, Marco Battaglia, Monika Künzler-Deon, Walter Lenggenhager and Anna Marie Wirz-Kupper for their particular support for the organisation and administration, Robert Steiger and Karoline Mueller-Stahl for their comprehensive readership, Stefan Zopp for his support from the AJN office in Lucerne.

Gallery of Architecture Lucerne, August 28, 1998

Katalog der Ausstellung / Catalogue of the Exhibition
Architekturgalerie Luzern
26. September bis 25. Oktober 1998

Herausgeber / Editor: Edition Architekturgalerie Luzern

Architekturgalerie Luzern
Luca Deon, Toni Häfliger, Heinz Wirz
Projektleitung Ausstellung und Katalog / Exhibition and Catalogue Coordinator: Luca Deon, Toni Häfliger
Konzept Ausstellung / Exhibition Concept: Jean Nouvel, Brigitte Métra
Konzept und Gestaltung Katalog / Concept and Design Catalogue: Jeanne-Marie Sens & Hubert Tonka, Paris
Koordination im Atelier Jean Nouvel / Coordination in the Jean Nouvel Studio: Charlotte Kruk
Fotos / Photographs: Jean Nouvel
Textbearbeitung / Editing: Sergio Cavero
Translation into English: Rebecca Lyon, Barry Stanton, Lausanne
Translation into German: Brigitta Neumeister-Taroni, Irene Bisang, Zürich
Translation into French (editorial): Thomas de Kayser, Paris
Druckvorstufe und Druck / Printing: Sticher Printing AG, Luzern

A CIP catalogue record for this book is available from the Library of Congress, Washington D.C., USA

Deutsche Bibliothek – CIP-Einheitsaufnahme
[Jean Nouvel, Concert Hall Luzern] Jean Nouvel, Concert Hall, Konzertsaal, Salle de Concert Luzern : [Katalog der Ausstellung Architekturgalerie Luzern, 26. September bis 25. Oktober 1998] / [Projektleitung Ausstellung und Katalog: Luca Deon ; Toni Häfliger]. - Basel ; Boston ; Berlin : Birkhäuser, 1999
ISBN 3-7643-5995-1 (Basel...)
ISBN 0-8176-5995-1 (Boston)

This work is subject to copyright. All rights reserved, whether the whole or part of the material is concerned, specifically the rights of translation, reprinting, re-use of illustrations, recitation, broadcasting, reproduction on microfilms or in other ways, and storage in data banks. For any kind of use permission of the copyright owner must be obtained.

© 1998 Edition Architekturgalerie Luzern, Rosenberghöhe 4, CH-6004 Luzern
Birkhäuser – Publishers for Architecture, P.O. Box 133, CH-4010 Basel, Switzerland
© Fotos / Photographs: Jean Nouvel

Printed on acid-free paper produced of chlorine-free pulp. TCF ∞
Printed in Switzerland
ISBN 3-7643-5995-1
ISBN 0-8176-5995-1
9 8 7 6 5 4 3 2 1